AS A WATCHMAN WAITS...

by Simon Cockshutt

"I wait for the Lord more than a watchman waits for the morning."

— PSALM 130:6 NIV

FOREWORD

The purpose of this little book is to be a trigger for a reflection on your life. It is meant to be picked up and put down again after only a short period. It is not a book that you would read through all in one sitting. But you could read it daily for a while. It is up to you. Some of the thoughts you may recognise as having been originally written for my blog.

With all good wishes from Simon

As A Watchman Waits… Copyright © 2019 by Simon Cockshutt. All Rights Reserved.

All rights reserved. No part of this book may be reproduced in any form or by any electronic or mechanical means including information storage and retrieval systems, without permission in writing from the author. The only exception is by a reviewer, who may quote short excerpts in a review.

Cover designed by Cover Designer

Passages marked NIV® are from THE HOLY BIBLE, NEW INTERNATIONAL VERSION
Copyright © 1973, 1978, 1984 by International Bible Society®
Used by permission. All rights reserved worldwide.

Printed on demand by Amazon

First Printing: January 2019
Independently Published

ISBN- 9781728864020

BREATH

Today I learnt that I take about 17,000 breaths a day. Most of those breaths are taken unconsciously. Breathe in, breathe out happens without me being particularly aware of it. The body is a strange and wonderful thing. The design or thoughtfulness of its construction is amazing. I came into the world over 64 years ago. Naked, probably crying I came. Somehow expelled from a womb where I hadn't been breathing air. Umbilical cord cut and then the shock of breathing in the new air of life. Ever since then, breath in, breath out.

Since then I have acquired possessions, which I have either then lost again or worn out. Or even disliked and thrown away. I don't currently own any possessions that I had on the day of my birth. Apart that is my body. If indeed you own your body or consciousness. Is it a gift or on loan? My mother and father should know but neither can I ask today.

Since then I have loved and lost. Lost and loved, many people. Lived many places. All the time, breath in, breath out. Heart beating. Some people I have been friends with and loved a very long time. My sisters have known me the longest.

I feel I must have had a creator. My mother and father co-operative with God's materials brought me into being. As I said, all the stuff or the possessions that were man-made have passed. The constant is my body that grew cell upon cell in my mother's womb. Heart beating.

Breath of God breathe on me. These morning thoughts are bringing me to the knowledge of how fragile and precious our life is. And yet my breathing is happening as I write without my conscious intervention.

Dear God, I thank you for the gift of my life and my love. Help me to renew my commitment to life, to live in love and to the fullest. Breath of God, breathe on me and the town where I live. Send your creative Holy Spirit to make us more for you and your kindness. Amen

THIS IS THE WAY WALK IN IT!

> This is what the LORD says: "Stand at the crossroads and look; ask for the ancient paths, ask where the good way is, and walk in it, and you will find rest for your souls." Jeremiah 6:16

We are all going somewhere with our lives. What is happening to us is always driving us in one direction or another. We never truly stand still. Do you ever wonder if there is a way forward out of your situation?

I was chatting to some work colleagues yesterday in the kitchen. We were joking about the national lottery, and one guy was saying how wonderful it would be to win it. But he was joking that he would have to give some money to his wife, his children, and his dog before they would let him enjoy any!

Buying a lottery ticket is a bit like buying a ticket for a dream. But a dream that lasts only to the next draw before it is dashed. But for one pound you can have a little bit of hope. And we all need a bit of hope in our lives.

I have discovered another source of hope, and it doesn't require money. For a while now, I have been a follower of a way that has a hope and a reality at the end of it. It is a way that gradually changes me for the better, and that lifts my spirits and lets me begin to encounter peace!

Thousands of years ago the prophet Isaiah wrote this passage "the Lord longs to be gracious to you; therefore he will rise up to show you compassion. For the LORD is a God of justice. How gracious he will be when you cry for help! As soon as he hears, he will answer you. Although the Lord gives you the bread of adversity and the water of affliction, your teachers will be hidden no more; with your own eyes you will see them. Whether you turn to the right or to the left, your ears will hear a voice behind you, saying, "This is the way; walk in it."

This gives us the impression that God is there to be interacted with. In my experience that is certainly true although we need to be listening in order to catch the Holy Spirit speaking into our lives.

God can sometimes guide us
- through the words of a stranger or friend
- through the words in the bible
- through life circumstances

- through the world he created
and sometimes he wants our response!

By following the ancient paths or ways, we are following well-trodden routes into the heart of God. Why go another less direct way!? Why go through the thicket and get caught in brambles when the path is there all along? I am inviting you to travel with me on that way that leads to God.

Dear Lord, guide us to that which makes us whole.
Send your Spirit again to our lives so that we are
renewed and strengthened. Amen

TAKE NOTHING FOR THE JOURNEY

> These were his instructions: "Take nothing for the journey except a staff--no bread, no bag, no money in your belts." Mark 6:8 (NIV)

When Jesus sent out the twelve disciples, he told them "take nothing for the journey." An extraordinary statement to people going on a journey. Even when I go bird watching, I put a muesli bar in my pocket! Yet they were doing far more than a hike. He also gave them other instructions too, and the full passage is to be found at Mark 6:8. But the bit I want to concentrate on today is the Jehovah Jireh nature of what Jesus says. Jehovah Jireh means "The Lord will provide." Jesus instruction to take no food was given because he was sending the twelve on a mission where they were going to rely on God to provide what they needed.

For us to approach God, we don't need to have anything other than ourselves. We don't need anything in advance. We don't need to wait until we are good enough or old enough. We don't even have to wait until we have finished giving up our addictions. For us to approach God all we need is ourselves and the willingness to turn our attention towards him. I invite you to do that today. You will find that Jehovah Jireh will provide for you too. All you need to do is turn your face him. It's good to be free of distractions, telly etc. but if you are in a place where you can't stop them, you can still approach God.

God is loving and wants to be able to bless you he has said "Call to me, and I will answer you" I want you to know that this promise is for you also. He is waiting to bring you peace.

As St James put it "Draw near to God and he will draw near to you."

You can speak to him in your own words as you would a friend. Or if you like, you can borrow the words below. When we approach God, it changes us. It can either be gradual or immediate. But somehow, we are changed for the better. I want my faith to strengthen you and for you to share something wonderful that I know about.

Dear God, you search me, and you know me, I ask you to make yourself known to me today. As it says in the Psalm "When my bones were being formed, carefully put together in my mother's womb, when I was growing there in secret, you knew that I was there. You saw me before I was born. The days allotted to me have all been recorded in your book." You know me as I am and as I would like to be, and your love as God is unconditional. Help me to take steps to be a better person. Touch my life with your loving kindness. Amen

THE WHITE STONE

For some years now, I have been carrying in my travel bible a small white stone. This is something that I have chosen to do as a reminder.

The longer in the tooth you get, the more you need to have things to keep you on track in your life. You think you know stuff, but sometimes you have known it so long that you wonder if you do really know it at all.

When I unzip this travel bible sometimes the stone falls out in front of me. It is very flat, I picked it up on a beach, so it has been smoothed by the sea, so at other times it can be found as a placeholder.

So, the significance is that it reminds me that by Jesus death and resurrection the price has been paid for me. I am acquitted before God. It reminds me that I am redeemed of the Lord. And that daily I should remember to live like a redeemed person. In the New Testament at Revelation 2.17, there is a reference to a white stone. It is thought that the writer of that book had in mind that when you stood before a judge for sentencing, he would signal his verdict by picking out either a white or black stone. If he picked a white stone, it meant that you were acquitted and free to go on your way. If the judge of your life has shown you the white stone, you are a new creation, as it says in Isaiah 'redeemed of the Lord.'

I am the kind of person who enjoys and needs the visual and this seemingly small thing helps to keep me on track. It is many years since I was brought to the decision point about God. Years since I said 'yes, Jesus I believe and want to make you Lord of my life.' but that decision has been the single most important thing I have done in my life. It has opened me to inner healing that I didn't think was possible.

Now I have this freedom I need to use it wisely and keep hold of it. As St Paul reminds us in the book of Galatians "Christ has set us free! Stand then as free people, and do not allow yourselves to become slaves again" (GNB Galatians 5:1)

Of course, in many ways, it is just a stone. But it is a reminder.

*I pray for you this day that the Lord will bless you
and lead you into a greater understanding of his
great love for you*

HAVE YOUR ROOTS AND FOUNDATION IN LOVE!

I had a lovely trip to Wakehurst Place a couple of years back with some of my sisters and just had to take a picture of this tree. It's amazing, isn't it? Doing it's level best to nurture itself and to survive. What you can't see in the photo was that on the rock was a tiny crevice filled with a bit of dirt and water. And that was proving just enough to let the tree grow just so far. But I can imagine that it will only reach and grow so far before it becomes too heavy for its delicate little roots and falls off.

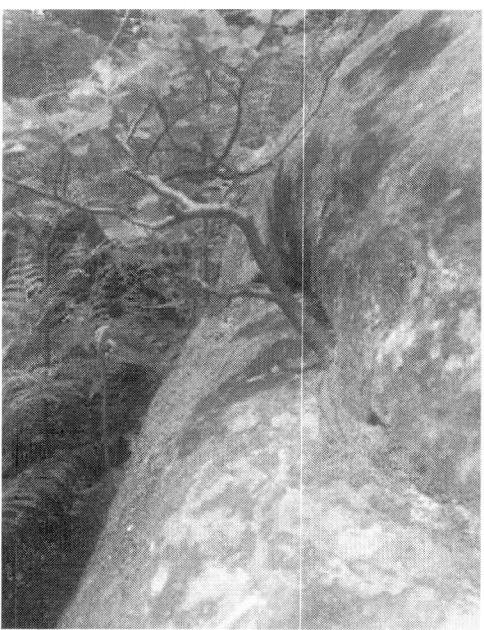

On the other hand, in Christchurch Park in Ipswich, I saw this fine specimen of a tree. Look how wonderful the roots are in comparison. This tree has been here for years and is likely to be around for quite a few years more.

It struck me that this is a bit like what happens to us in life. Now of course about some things we don't have a choice they are decided for us by circumstances and other forces like our parents. But it doesn't do to hold them responsible for everything, does it? Therefore, the big question is, do we take the time, and I suppose trouble, to nurture our own lives? And is what we do really nurturing? I know that is a wide-reaching question and that as we are composed of body, soul and spirit, it might set our minds running in different directions. But let's forget about the body for the moment and think about our spirit. I am convinced that what has really nurtured me in my life is the love that I have received from people. Some of it totally undeserved. But to be loved and to love is a refreshing experience. It lifts us and renews us. Whereas if we choose something death giving like sin or drugs the opposite of nurture takes place. And we can become like the tree in the first picture ready to drop off our perch!

Now God loved us first! This lovely passage from St Paul's letter to the Ephesians reminds us that the true source for nourishment in our lives is the love that comes from God.

"I ask God from the wealth of his glory to give you power through his Spirit to be strong in your inner selves, and I pray that Christ will make his home in your hearts through faith. I pray that you may have your roots and foundation in love, so that you, together with all God's people, may have the power to understand how broad and long, how high and deep, is Christ's love."

> *Dear Father God, I pray that each of us may come to know you a bit better and be able to respond to the love that you have for us, invade our lives with your gentle, life-giving, Holy Spirit blessing us and renewing us, please make us like a well-watered garden - growing in your love daily. Amen*

COME BACK TO THE SHEEPFOLD?

At nearly every funeral I have ever been to Psalm 23 has been sung. Known as the 'Lord is my shepherd,' it is also used as the theme song for the Vicar of Dibley. I have been re-reading the words and trying to figure out what it is that makes it one of the most asked for hymns at funerals. I believe that it is because it is so very consoling. It reminds us of the relationship between us and God our creator. Saying that God is like a Shepherd in the way that he cares for us. It is a way of describing the relationship that still works for those that live in the country. But we need to be aware in biblical times the shepherd would have lived with their sheep for months at a time.

The psalm is saying that we are sheep to God's shepherding. Whether we view that as a flattering or unflattering thought it still tells us about how we depend on God for so many things. A good shepherd will look after his sheep from birthing them as lambs onwards. Finding water for them. Finding good pastures for them. Leading them to shelter when it is stormy. Rescuing them when they get caught in thorn bushes or stuck on a crag. The flip side is a bad, uncaring shepherd could destroy his flock through lack of care.

We as sheep need to listen to the voice of the shepherd calling us. They say sheep literally do know their shepherd's voice. If they don't, they can perish.

Some things in life bring us up short. Funerals being one of them, then we can find ourselves asking am I living the way that I should? What will happen if I carry on like this? We have but one shot at our life. But all of us are capable with the help of God of making changes, making mid-course corrections. Maybe we need to let the shepherd find us again. To learn once again to hear the voice of a shepherd on my life. Calming and correcting me and leading me to nourishment.

Dear Lord, shepherd of my soul. I ask your blessings on my life. At times I have been like a sheep without a shepherd wandering without direction. Help my restless heart to find the way back to you. Fill me afresh with your peace and lead me onwards. Amen

CHOOSE LIFE

> Those that live in Christ are called into a way of living that is led by the Holy Spirit. Consider these words from St Paul "no longer do we serve in the old way of a written law, but in the new way of the Spirit" Romans 7.6

And Jesus by his life, death and resurrection brought us into a new way of having an experience of God in our life. Referring to the time we are now living in, he said, "God is Spirit, and only by the power of his Spirit can people worship him as he really is" John 4.24

Jesus ushered in a change in the way people think about religion. In fact, he almost abolished the word itself! Instead, he revealed much about the inner mind of God that tells us of his heart for us his creation. Jesus speaks to us with a clarity that goes to the core of our being. Sometimes these words can hit right to the nub of something we are wrestling with. Yesterday, for example, I had been thinking about sin. And the choice we have every day between the two ways, as St Paul puts it, only one of the ways leads to that which will make us more complete.

A close friend of mine dropped by for a chat and a cuppa. We ended up chatting about all sorts of things and something led us to these words of Christ "whoever believes in the Son is not judged; but whoever does not believe has already been judged, because he has not believed in God's only Son. This is how the judgement works : the light has come into the world, but people love the darkness rather than the light, because their deeds are evil. Anyone who does evil things hates the light and will not come to the light, because he does not want his evil deeds to be shown up. But whoever does what is true comes to the light in order that the light may show that what he did was in obedience to God." John 3.18 (GNB).

That passage made me realise that it is not God who condemns me, it is my actions. Every day I can choose either to bless or to curse. To Love or to hate. To forgive or to store up the pain of unresolved anger. To live in the light or hide my sins in the darkness. And, when I have sinned sometimes, I can't bring myself into the presence of that which is good.

But we have a God who will forgive us if we ask. A God who loves the repentant sinner.

Dear Lord, help me to choose to love on a daily basis. Help me to do away with the things of the darkness. Bring me inch by inch into the fullness of your love. Amen

GOD DELIGHTS IN SHOWING MERCY

One of my preoccupations, since I moved to Ipswich, is which rubbish bin I should put out on a Monday evening. I always have to look it up as I can never remember whether to put my black or blue bin out.

Do you ever wonder what it would be like if we could de-junk our personal lives from the burdens that we carry? Wouldn't it be lovely to be able to put our emotional baggage out for collection?

Some of that feeling we have of emotional baggage comes from having unresolved sin in our lives. I want you to listen to some words from the prophet Micah that reveal a wonderful image of God. Here they are:

"What god can compare with you: taking fault away, pardoning crime, not cherishing anger forever but delighting in showing mercy? Once more have pity on us, tread down our faults, to the bottom of the sea throw all our sins. Grant Jacob your faithfulness, and Abraham your mercy, as you swore to our fathers from the days of long ago." Jerusalem Bible

That sounds like a God that cares for us and wants us to succeed, doesn't it? And what a beautiful image "tread down our faults to the bottom of the sea."

Before we go further with that thought, we need to ask ourselves what is sin? In the original language of the NewTestament, the Greek word 'hamartia' is used. Literally translated this means to 'miss the mark.' Sin is when we deliberately choose to miss the mark. Where we deliberately choose a bad action instead of a good or neutral action. Another way of looking at it is that sin is when we choose to be unloving in the way we act. Now there are various levels of harm caused by sin. A major, or grave, one would be to murder someone. Obviously, the harm in that is colossal. A minor sin in comparison is when we tell a white lie. But even that has a knock-on effect.

St Paul says that sin unchecked leads to death. I believe that he means spiritual death, but he might equally be warning of physical death. We can quite see that the cumulative results of a series of negative actions could lead us into the sort of angry conflict where death ensues. Sometimes inevitably one evil thing leads to another.

Some sins break national laws as well as spiritual laws. It is worth us thinking about the following passage from St Paul "The commandments are summed up in the one command, "Love your neighbour as you love yourself." If you love someone you will never do them wrong; to love then is to obey the whole law." Romans 13:10 - Surely this means that love should be the yardstick by which we need to measure our actions?

The thing about the Christian faith is that it is about redemption. It doesn't lead us to an awareness of sin and then leave us 'high and dry' to wallow in our misery. God through Jesus offers us a new beginning. A way out of sin, a new way of forgiveness that comes from God.

God wants us to be happy and fulfilled people who have put darkness behind us. He can bring us to a stage where we are aware of our sins. When that happens, we need to then turn to him and ask what we need to do put things right. It could be, for example, that we need to forgive someone or ask them to forgive us. That forgiveness then opens us to receive God's forgiveness. The fact that we are trying to make amends allows a spiritual dynamic to happen.

Now the great thing is that we can access this grace gift at any time. We don't have to wait until the one day in two weeks when the bin men come. God comes out to meet us on the road and is prepared at any time to "tread down our faults to the bottom of the sea."

Dear Lord, help me to identify what in my life needs changing. Show me how that change can happen. Give me courage and insight to take the steps that I need to. Help me to bless and not to curse. To build and not to destroy. May your Spirit come to strengthen me, Amen

FAITHFUL IN SMALL THINGS

Now Debs and I were discussing the various versions of CSI on the telly the other day. Trying to think which our favourite was. After a bit of banter, I told Debs that the lead character in CSI Miami Horatio Caine is my favourite because he "wears his integrity like a blanket" as the psalm says. There are several examples where he goes beyond the call of duty to help a victim. Exhibiting a kindness that goes beyond his role as a member of the police. He almost invariably addresses hardened criminals as "my friend," even when pointing out to them that he has got them banged to rights. For an example of his kindness did you see the episode where the witness to a crime had learning difficulties? There was a kind of tender-hearted compassion thing going on.

I know it is just fiction. However, storytelling has been important to humans for thousands of years.

The conversation with Debs seems to have a link in my head to two other passages from scripture about integrity that have come to the forefront of my attention.

> They do not distinguish between the holy and the common; they teach that there is no difference between the unclean and the clean; and they shut their eyes to the keeping of my Sabbaths, so that I am profaned among them. Ezekiel 22:26 NIV

and

> I know, my God, that you test the heart and are pleased with integrity. All these things I have given willingly and with honest intent. And now I have seen with joy how willingly your people who are here have given to you. 1 Chronicles 29:17 NIV

All this I suppose set me of thinking, where or how do we start to be like that man Horatio?

I think our life it has to start with small things. Remember where Jesus says, "Whoever is faithful in small matters will be faithful in large ones; whoever is dishonest in small matters will be dishonest in large ones." Luke 16.10 GNB

The psalm really does say in the translation I use "wear your integrity like a blanket" which I believe means your integrity should protect you from the insidious temptations that come our way. That thought goes nicely with somewhere else in the psalms where it says, "shake your hand lest it contains a bribe." This prompts us that we need to remember to be faithful in the small things.

So, we need a foundation to build on. Maybe that is enough to think on today? Except to add that daily repentance helps. It is better to do several little midcourse corrections rather than one jarring sharp turnaround.

Dear Lord, you search me, and you know me. Help me to be faithful in small things and tenderhearted, let my "yes" be "yes" and my "no" be "no." Give me words that build up. Amen

THOUGHTS ABOUT IONA

This little island has had a significant impact on Christianity for two main reasons.

First, it is where St Columba's landed in AD 563, bringing with him Christianity to the Scottish people.

Secondly, it is the spiritual home of the Wildgoose Community. A community that has been a blessing for many people since it was founded 1938.

It was like a pilgrimage for us, rising early on Friday and heading off to be sure to get the 7am flight to Glasgow. Then by car and ferry and many birding stops to Mull and beyond to the tiny island of Iona. On the way, we saw the awesome beauty of God's creation, including Otters swimming, an Osprey flying, and a Buzzard perched so that we could see him clearly in all his finery through our telescope. Creation too is God's message to us about the Father's love for variety and beauty.

At our first prayer stop, we had a reading etc. from a book we had brought with us.

My heart was struck by these words, that seemed to be there to prepare my heart for marriage, "It is possible to travel alone. But the good traveller knows that the journey is human life and needs company." The very word companion itself means the one who eats the same bread. Debs, of course, is my companion, friend and lover! All these things are necessary for a marriage to work, with the grace of God's Holy Spirit too in generous measure.

And from Jeremiah we learnt about our new heart:

> "This is the covenant I will make with the people of Israel after that time," declares the Lord. "I will put my law in their minds and write it on their hearts. I will be their God, and they will be my people. No longer will they teach their neighbour, or say to one another, 'Know the Lord,' because they will all know me, from the least of them to the greatest," declares the Lord. "For I will forgive their wickedness and will remember their sins no more." Jeremiah 31:33-34 NIV

The House of Prayer we stayed in was a beautiful, welcoming home thanks to Sister Jean. And for two days we became family with the other visitors. Two lovely American women Pat and Marie and two Norwegian Dominican monks Haavar and Arnfinn. Eating breakfast and dinner together. Talking, sharing and with good humour together.

At this meeting at the crossroads was an interesting mix of Christian people, proving that there is fellowship across the divides. We can all be one just as Jesus asks.

This will be a long if I tell you everything. So let's just today think about kindness.

I have mentioned in previous pages "the loving kindness which is the heart of our God "

On the descent into Columba's Bay, we experienced the unexpected kindness of a stranger - who appeared from nowhere and offered to take a picture of the three amigos. We exchanged brief friendly words and the information that we were on a rather eccentric Bucks weekend involving prayer and birding. She seemed shy but did say what she was doing. She then went on ahead stopped in her tracks and came back. She said that she wanted to give me, and Debs two green stones known as Columba's Tears - she did this and then hurried on her way. Needless to say, I thanked her for her kindness. I was quite touched - the unexpected kindness of strangers does indeed reach the heart very quickly.

So, for me, the predominant theme of the weekend was that God was telling me that he wants me to learn his kindness. To not be afraid to accept it from others, but also to be more consistent in my attempts to show it to other people. Especially while in London - that busy place - oh God let me help the traveller and to see them through your eyes. And thank you for the humour and patience that John and Chris shared with me.

We are but fallible people like clay pots! "We have this treasure in jars of clay to show that this all-surpassing power is from God and not from us." That is if our intentions are good, God will cover our weakness.

Dear God, please help me to be more consistent in the practice of kindness and help me to recognise the need in others and do what I am able to help them.

ABOUT MARRIAGE

As preparation for Saturday, I have been thinking this morning about 1 Corinthians 13 and reading something I wrote about it a while ago for a niece of mine.

Funnily enough, we decided not to use this reading at our wedding. But I love it so briefly here are some thoughts on it.

The highest calling that each of us has is to live a life that is filled with love. What else could make us happy? It is as if we have a thirst inside us that only love could satisfy. We humans need to receive love and to give love. Whether it be as a parent to child, child to parent, friend to friend or of course the love that exists between a married couple.

Christine Aged 9 said that in a restaurant "It is love - if they order one of those desserts that are on fire. They like to order them because it is just like how their hearts are, on fire."

I agree with this young lady our hearts do need to be on fire for the one we have chosen as our marriage partner.

We should as it says in the bible "live a lover's life" - to be passionate in our love is what we need. Even if it makes our partner giggle! Better to be passionate than 2 dimensional. We should give them our best! As far as we are able, within our capacity, we should love at full tilt, with no reservations.

We should not be afraid to serve them, and they should also not be afraid to serve us in turn. I remember a poster that I had on my wall for a while when I was a young man, "Where love rules, there is no will to power" it said. By serving our loved one and looking to the others need we are purifying our love of the distortions that power can bring if used wrongly. We need the creative power of the Holy Spirit in our marriage.

Dear Lord, you know all about me and love me anyway. Help me to be real in my loving, help me to learn how to love - Amen

BE THOU MY VISION

The wonderful thing about our God is that he has an individual plan for each one of us. A plan for us to be happy and fulfilled. We are happiest when we can find that plan and live by it. When we discern it and live by it, we are people of vision.

Through careful listening to the Spirit and hearing it speaking in many ways and in all gentleness into our lives, we can get a sense of rightness about the way ahead.

When this happens, we should make a record of it; We should write it down as Habakkuk says:

> The LORD gave me this answer: "Write down clearly on tablets what I reveal to you so that it can be read at a glance. Put it in writing, because it is not yet time for it to come true. But the time is coming quickly, and what I show you will come true. It may seem slow in coming, but wait for it; it will certainly take place, and it will not be delayed." (Habakkuk 2:2-3 GNT)

I think we are told to "write down" our vision for two reasons
- so we can be faithful to it
- so we can remember it in good times as well as bad times

In Proverbs, it warns us (rather starkly I think!) that if we do not have a vision for our lives, we will perish!

Debs and I are working on our vision for the House of Prayer that we feel God is telling us to establish. It will be a while before we have finished listening to God on this.

However, if you don't mind reading some unedited text - this is what he said to us about integrity in ministry after we went to church last Sunday in the Queensland resort of Caloundra, I am leaving the church unnamed. It is, more or less, a prayer, so read it as such, when we pray the words come with pauses and imperfections!

Purify our intentions, Lord,

Purify our church,

Let our first witness be our love for people, our genuine concern for them, and make our love sincere

What you want is "Love not sacrifice."

Help us to be faithful in small things

To wear our integrity "like a blanket."

Help us not to judge other people but at the same time have discernment between good and evil.

Let us only have "the debt of mutual love" and let us NEVER encourage others to use their VISA card to go into debt to give to us.

Let us not be "over righteous," you require us only to be righteous and to love with a "humble, contrite heart."

Inch by inch claim our hearts O Lord, help us to allow you to do it quicker than even that if we dare to let you!

You are our Lord, dear Jesus, and you are also our brother and our friend. Anoint us again with your love this day, send your Holy Spirit to us again to strengthen and renew us. Help us to desire, not worthless things but instead to desire only you. Amen.

THE GREAT SOUTHLAND OF THE HOLY SPIRIT

Before this latest trip to Australia, I had never heard the expression "The Great Southland of the Holy Spirit" - and then in the run-up to our little time of prayer on the beach, two people referred to the phrase in prayer with me.

It seems that the Latin words "Terra Australis del Espiritu Sanctu" was the name given to the Great South Land by Spanish explorer Pedro Fernandez de Quiros in 1606.

Translated into English "Great South Land of the Holy Spirit" is one of the titles for this great land mass that what we now know as the nation of Australia.

I have been praying about this, and I feel God has been saying to me that Pedro Fernandez had a Word of Knowledge when he named Australia that way. Sometimes the Holy Spirit reveals to us something that we speak out, and we think "where did that come from!?" - I know from the prayer that I have received here in Australia that others too have already seen a significance in the name.

I think I dare to say that we are on the verge of a tipping point of the Holy Spirit that will pour out from this land to the ends of the earth. This is something I only know in my spirit but heed this preceding utterance of a mortal man. Said in obedience to God.

Dear Lord, we know that for you anything is possible and that the "light is stronger than the darkness" - kindle once more in us the fire of your love. Give us once again a knowledge of your great love for us. Overwhelm us with it and give us a true understanding of your love for the whole of the world. Amen

YEAR OF GRACE

On Saturday, 9 June 2012 we arrived back in Ipswich UK after a long journey.

Last week I wrote "I think I dare to say that we are on the verge of a tipping point of the Holy Spirit that will pour out from this land (meaning Australia) to the ends of the earth. This is something I only know in my spirit but heed this preceding utterance of a mortal man. Said in obedience to God." - I thought in a way I had been stupid and headstrong in writing that - The following day I discovered that maybe I was not so stupid after all!

I visited Brisbane Cathedral and hung around for mass, because I like to do that sort of thing, pray and listen, I discovered that the Bishop there had written a pastoral letter to his flock declaring that Pentecost should mark a "Year of Grace" - this is an excerpt from his letter:

> "But the plot thickens. When God comes down to us in Jesus, we prefer to run away – saying as we do, "No thanks, I can do it by myself". We would rather die in our own way than live in God's way. We would rather starve at the foot of the mountain than allow God to carry us to the feast on the summit. That's the underlying attitude that becomes sin in our life. But God is not so easily put off, because Jesus, the Good Shepherd, comes looking for the run-away sheep. When he finds them, he puts them on his shoulders and carries them up the mountain where they can enjoy the restful waters and the fresh green pastures of the feast. And all of this is done out of the free and extravagant love that we call "grace", which is the very heart of the Christian life.

He continued, "This Pentecost Sunday we begin what we're calling the Year of Grace. This will be like a time of retreat for the whole Church in Australia – a time to refocus on what really matters, a time to rediscover the heart of the Christian life.

We can't earn the almost incredible love of God, but we don't have to. It's given to the unworthy as a free gift. All they have to do is accept it. But that can be harder than it sounds, given our tendency to insist that we can do it all ourselves."

If a whole national church is going to pray for a year of grace, It will happen! And it will pour out over other nations. Debs and I found the Holy Spirit working in Brisbane and also with the COC church at Bribie Island where we experienced an amazingly prayerful service. The same Holy Spirit is working in different churches.

Gracious God,
You have blessed this ancient land
with many gifts, especially its people.
We thank you for the Year of Grace,
a time to start afresh from Christ.
You invite us to contemplate the face of Jesus your Son,
that we may experience a new wave of grace,
and that the light of Christ may burn more brightly
in our lives.
Attune our hearts and minds
to the presence of your Holy Spirit,
that our Church may be transformed,
our relationships be healed,
and our nation grow in compassion and justice.
With the intercession of St Mary MacKillop,
who showed us new ways of living the Gospel,
we make our prayer
through Christ our Lord. Amen.
Mary, Help of Christians, pray for us.
overcome

WHERE YOU FALL YOU CAN GROW!

There can be moments in our life where we despair. Where life seems so bleak that we can't see the way ahead or the way through the crisis even.

In those situations, we can take comfort from the following passage from the prophet Jeremiah.

> The LORD said to me, "Go down to the potter's house, where I will give you my message." So I went there and saw the potter working at his wheel. Whenever a piece of pottery turned out imperfect, he would take the clay and make it into something else. (Jeremiah 18: 1-4 GNT)

We know that Jeremiah thought that God is like the potter and that we are like the clay when we surrender our lives to him. When we are imperfect, we can be made into something else if we surrender to God. Made into something better!

Years and years ago I had a nervous breakdown. I was in a very bleak position but went anyway to some friends to be prayed with. I think that I thought to myself that "well it can't do any harm." To my surprise, I encountered a moment of grace with God and started to get better. One of my friends read the Jeremiah passage to me. After and during my recovery I cherished rereading that passage from Jeremiah. It still means a lot to me when I hear the phrase "Go down to the potter's house."

John and I were walking in a wood yesterday, and we found this massive oak tree that had fallen to the ground. It must have been ages ago that it fell because growing from the tree were all these vertical shoots of new trees coming up.

When I saw the tree lying like that horizontally, I thought here is something that has weathered disaster and is being renewed. The secret of this trees regrowth is that it is still able to draw nourishment through its capillaries and use that nourishment to fuel growth. We can be like that tree too. Even when we have fallen in life, for whatever reason, if we can recognise that God is a source of nourishment we can turn to him and be replenished.

If we put our roots out to God, we can draw strength from him. It might take time, but we can become something new. In listening to God, we might find that he tells us to change something in our life. Maybe to give something up that is harmful or to start doing something. For each one of us, the catalyst to growth or healing might be different. But as it says in scripture "You will seek me and find me when you seek me with all your heart" – God allows himself to be found when we look for him.

Dear Lord, I come to you today in my brokenness,
help me to listen to you and draw nourishment
from you. I seek only life, teach me what I need to
change to find peace of mind and happiness in you.
Amen

BE CAREFUL HOW YOU THINK

What does today hold for you? What has gone on for you or what is about to happen? Whatever our belief system it is important to know which way is up on any particular day. If we wander around like a loon in a haze, or interfering in things, and never settling down to do something, we will just be static noise on the soundtrack of history. Just how do we make the best of our lives? How do we do being "me" the best way that we can?

Consider this advice from the book of Proverbs.

> Be careful how you think; your life is shaped by your thoughts. Never say anything that isn't true. Have nothing to do with lies and misleading words. Look straight ahead with honest confidence; don't hang your head in shame. Plan carefully what you do, and whatever you do will turn out right. Avoid evil and walk straight ahead. Don't go one step off the right way.
> Proverbs 4:23-27 GNT

Oh! To be a person with the passion of "honest confidence" who is living and loving in the freedom of the Holy Spirit. That is my dream. This passage is about being someone with discernment, someone who can grow into the things of God.

As St Paul puts it, we have the choice between the two paths in our life. A choice between Good and Evil. When it says "Be careful how you think; your life is shaped by your thoughts" - The inkling or precursor of Good or Evil comes from our thoughts. What we think we so easily end up doing. This is why we need an understanding of God's law of love in our hearts. When we choose to love, we choose good, and our lives are enriched. If we choose to do the opposite our lives are impoverished.

Our actions have a cause and effect on other people. Very few of our actions are totally neutral. But that shouldn't scare us. But it should make us want to seize God's creative power for the positive. The power to bless and not to curse. The joy of compassionate tenderhearted love in our lives.

So dear reader! Seize this day be wise in the use of your time. Try to be able to recognise when it is God's given time to act. Look for moments when it is time to bless! Even if it is time to bless a complete stranger. Or time to bless our spouse or friend or relative. Bless doesn't just mean words or prayers it means, actions and listenings. Taking part in the ordinary and somehow converting it into special moments. The bible has two words for time

- Chronos = the time that we have to spend, elapsed time so to speak
- Kairos = special God chosen moments, times of blessing, times of Grace that come when we co-author them with God, when we co-operate with him and cease to struggle!

When we don't have clear thinking in our life, we have instead

- Chaos = life jumbled up and messy

God does pardon our errors and loves us despite them. We are given a chance to redeem our past. I am living proof of that. An unfinished work of a person being redeemed. Seeking the positive.

Dear Lord, send your inspiration into my thinking. Breathe your creative power into it and use me for your kingdom. Help me to build it here on earth. Teach me gently, or even strongly (!) how to tap into your love. Amen

IF WE LIVE WE LIVE FOR THE LORD, AND IF WE DIE WE DIE FOR THE LORD

In loving memory of my mother Jean who died on 3rd July 2009. The following is the homily I preached at her funeral:

The words from Romans "The life and death of each one of us has its influence on others, if we live, we live for the Lord, and if we die we die for the Lord." seem very appropriate for Jean's funeral.

Jean our mother, sister, grandma, great grandma and friend.

To know Jean was to know someone who had inherited a very strong Christian faith from her father. She did her best to put that faith into action. She wasn't a saint by any means but what she did understand was that at the heart of the Christian gospel is the overwhelming transforming power of love. To simply love other people has an influence. The kind of love a Christian has (they call it agape) simply does invite a response.

This isn't the eulogy – we will come to that later. I just want to try and explain what motivated my mother to be the person she was. If I understand correctly (and I think I do) her life's motivation came from knowing her father Harold Wesley Bardwell and knowing Jesus.

They say faith is caught not taught. She caught her faith from her father. And I think that she would want me to explain (briefly) about Faith Hope and Love.

St Paul famously said, "to have faith is to be sure of the things we hope for, to be certain of the things that we cannot see."

Faith is not a step into the dark. It is a step into the light. From the faith giving moment we go forward, shakily at first, like a child taking first steps. But the amazing thing is the more we walk in faith, the more steady we become and the more we experience God's love and the certainty that there is a God who cares about us. It is something that you have to do for yourself before you can be truly convinced about the truth of what I am saying. She was always supporting people in their faith. In quite a discreet and kind way. Always willing to chat about the difficult subjects and very sure Jean's certainty was that there is life after death.

She chose today's gospel and pretty much all the hymns we are singing. She wanted you to hear those words from Jesus " I am the resurrection and the life. Those who believe in me will live, even though they die; and those who live and believe in me will never die."

Jean had quite a few experiences that made her convinced that there was a life after death. That when she died her life would change but not end. We talked about it a lot over the last few months. When it came to it, she was ready to die and unshakeable in her faith. We can take consolation in that. She believed what Jesus said about the resurrection. I share that faith with her. Her great joy would be in you sharing it too.

She wouldn't want us to be especially sad at her passing and would want us to be glad for her in our tears. And she would want us to know love and to give and receive it today.

May your hearts be at peace. May you find consolation in your grief. May you find hope in the resurrection today as we celebrate the Life and love of Jean Frances Cockshutt.

LIVE BY THE SPIRIT

> Those who live as their human nature tells them to, have their minds controlled by what human nature wants. Those who live as the Spirit tells them to, have their minds controlled by what the Spirit wants. To be controlled by human nature results in death; to be controlled by the Spirit results in life and peace. (Romans 8:5-6 GNT)

I have been giving some thought to the renovation of my personal life. Asking myself what it means to walk daily in the Spirit. Without being antsy fancy just thinking what could be better in my life? However, remember God doesn't require us to be a stuffed shirt or without humour. If the three most important fruits of a Holy Spirit led life are Love, Peace and Joy then glumness has no place in Christianity!

What follows though is a rough guide to walking in the Spirit, which when followed will inevitably promote growth in the things of God and in our personal life. Try these components together for three months, and I guarantee that your interior life will change. I said previously that I had learnt over the years that Christianity is a relationship and not a religion. Well, listed below is what will help that relationship with God grow. Furthermore, your relationships with others will also change.

Regular daily prayer time changes us. Remember "to pray is to change."

Time spent in the Word feeds our spirit and challenges us. Read the bible because it is the "Word of God" and contains God's message for us which is relevant for all even to this moment.

Asking the Holy Spirit what he wants you to do today, sometimes it is only one thing – the Spirit rarely overwhelms us with demands.

Give up judging other people!

Ask God who you should be forgiving (also think about who you have offended and go to them asking to be forgiven).

Live in community! This is harder if you are housebound but if possible spend time with other Christians. Find people who are trying to grow up in the Lord and be with them. (it says in Proverbs "iron sharpens iron" and this is the community effect, it sharpens us so that we are more alert to the things of the Lord).

Meditating on the Our Father. There is a reason why Jesus told his disciples to pray using this prayer read/say it often, and you will start to get why.

All components to be taken daily as the master physician Doctor Jesus has directed us. Start out with at least 10 minutes a day and then eventually build it up to thirty minutes or more each day. Components can be taken in any order, but a good way to start is by reading a psalm out loud. Always talk to Jesus as you would a friend. Give time to listening too because in our pauses God can inspire us Follow this and I will talk in more detail about each of the steps above. But don't delay start today!

Dear Jesus, I desire my life to be different – renew in me your Holy Spirit so that I may grow in the things of God. Send your peace to my life. Give me a listening heart. Amen

LIVE BY THE SPIRIT (2) PRAYER

Last time I wrote "Regular daily prayer time changes us. Remember 'to pray is to change.'"

I promised to say more, so here it is! Let's deal with why we pray first. You can view prayer as a chance to be in God's presence. It is intentional face time with God. It begins with us choosing to come into His presence and making ourselves available. But why? To pray is to speak to God – as it says in the bible itself "Speak to God as you would a friend" (Exodus 33:11). I would add that you can speak to God as you would your very best friend. Telling Him the unedited version of your life! In doing this, I find that prayer very often brings peace to me although there are times when God like a true friend, gently challenges me with the truth. I find that I do a fair amount of telling God stuff, some asking, some praising God and then there is Listening.

Starting off in prayer can be the biggest challenge for us. Yet God always wants to hear from us. The danger is that we decide to wait until we can make our prayers fully formed and in doing this consequently hold back until we think we can be eloquent. The reality is that we have to start somewhere and that somewhere can be very faltering. I remember years back in the 1970s going to a weekly prayer group and being encouraged by the leader to pray out loud. For weeks at a time, all I could manage was one sentence here and there. But I began to realise that God was just as accepting of my one sentence prayers as those of the others.

To praise God is to tell him how great he is. If we look at the psalms we can see the praise language developing in a prayer context; we hear the psalmist say things like "the Lord is King, let the earth rejoice" or "blessed be the name of the Lord." Although we have heard those words many times out of habit or tradition, it is good to remind ourselves that we say things like that for two reasons. The main being that it reminds us that of the two of us God is definitely greater. God is worthy to be praised because he is our creator, and he made the universe and all that is in it. The second reason for praising God is that he likes it! It's just a fact!

Why or how do we change? I think it is a combination of the Holy Spirit gradually acting on our lives and melting our hearts making them more compassionate and also through prayer and being in a relationship with Jesus we are gradually challenged to be a bit different in our outlook and behaviour.

How did prayer start? Throughout faith history, going back thousands of years in the bible there are many recorded times of prayer. For our Jewish and

Christian ancestors, it was just an accepted part of everyday life, and many of their prayers are written in the bible and can be helpful for us to read.

Here is an example of a prayer of blessing from a father to a child "May the Lord bless you and take care of you, May the Lord be kind and gracious to you: May the Lord look on you with favour and give you peace" GNT Numbers 6:2

Jesus prayed as part of the natural rhythm of his life, and we need to be like that too. He would say to his disciples "come away with me to a quiet place" he gave us the "Our Father", and he promised us about prayer that "where two or three gather in my name, there am I with them."

I call you forward into prayer and into a relationship with God. May he bless you today as you read this, and may his spirit gently infuse your soul with the peace of Christ and his love. When I started writing this, there was really heavy rain. I stumbled across a passage which seemed to be like a word from God showing me his sense of humour but also teaching me something. "May my instruction soak in like the rain, and my discourse permeate like the dew, Like a downpour upon the grass, like a shower upon the crops. For I will sing the Lord's renown."

May the Lord be in our hearts and in our love today. Help us to step forward O Lord in prayer. Free us to praise you and listen to you. You are worthy to be praised. Amen

LIVE BY THE SPIRIT (3) TIME SPENT IN THE WORD

Time spent in the Word feeds our spirit and challenges us.

Sometimes God uses something earthly to teach you something heavenly! I remember in the 1970s in a Café style meeting when a young woman insisted on reading the bible to me, passage after passage, eventually literally sitting on my feet whilst she did so. She prayed that the Holy Spirit would fill me with a love for the Word. Her insistence and prayer have been answered. But it amuses me that God had to use an attractive woman to get my attention, so He could get the point through to me.

Now God may not be using that luxury this day with you, but chances are he will find some way in your life of speaking to your heart.

Let me assure you that it is my lived experience that there is power in the Word of God, the kind of heart-changing power that can only come from God himself.

For the sake of clarity, I will explain that when we talk about the Word, we mean "the Word of God" or the Bible. Christians believe that the bible is inspired by God - inspired in the sense that God has breathed spiritual power into it. It is a Spiritually true account of humankind's faith journey. But even more than that it tells of the life, death and resurrection of Jesus the Son of God. It gives us his teaching and many other messages, prayers and insights that can help us in our everyday life. It is also God's instruction manual for a fulfilled and happy life.

The Word helps us to "Live by the Spirit" because it reveals to us day by day the truth about God. To know more about God is to love him more. To know him is to understand him.

To start dwelling in the Word, you could experiment with praying with the scriptures open in front of you during your prayer time. What works for me is to read a passage out loud and then to pause praying for the Spirit to speak to my heart. I then re-read it looking for key phrases that speak to my heart. Quite often there are one sentence phrases in scripture that sum up the passage or open up its meaning. Some psalms have several. So, find in your passage one of these phrases and say it out loud a few times, dwelling on its meaning for you.

An example would be "where your treasure is, so too is your heart" which is from Matthew 6:19-24. Ask God what he wants to tell you in the sentence you have selected. Examine the different meanings it could have.

Debs and I tried this with Psalm 68 the other day, and we each got different things out of it and shared with each other. It led to quite a special time of the Spirit speaking to us. I for example reflected on the phrase that says God is, "a father for the fatherless" – which has been true in my life. I grew up in a household with an absent father. From time to time in my life, God has provided for me men who have had a father role with me. Good men, it has to be said, who could speak in wisdom to my life. Debs had, "Summon your power, God; show us your strength, our God, as you have done before." Sometimes we find things that encourage us. At other times things that challenge us. At other times steps to take in faith.

May Jesus be present to you today. May your life receive the blessing of Christ – the Holy One of God. May his gentle peace be with you, refreshing and renewing you. Amen

LIVE BY THE SPIRIT (4) ASKING

My focus today is on "Asking the Holy Spirit what he wants you to do today, sometimes it is only one thing - the Spirit rarely overwhelms us with demands."

It seems novel, doesn't it? To Live by the Spirit, you listen to it. So why do I find it hard to say to God - "send your Holy Spirit" or "Speak Lord your servant is listening?"

But remember "To be controlled by human nature results in death; to be controlled by the Spirit results in life and peace." Romans 8.6

Perhaps the answer is in conquering our human nature. Again, I would say this is not about turning our lives into a joyless dry landscape. The fruits of the Spirit are love, peace and joy. So, it stands to reason that when we live more by the Spirit, we have more and more of these things in our life. But to get to that stage, we need to take instructions "to develop a listening ear" for the sweet sound of the Lord's voice on our life saying, "this is the way walk in it." With the London 2012 Olympics playing out on our TV screens at present it is easy to draw the comparison to the training of athletes. Listening to an interview yesterday I heard described the training regime of a medal winner in swimming. In order to win you need to get in the water daily. I would say to you "wade in the Spirit's water daily."

In your prayer time pause and let the Spirits voice find it's a way to you in the peace. Give up the idea that the dialogue with God can happen in a five-minute slot that you assign to him first thing in the morning before you brush your teeth! Our God is a very demanding lover and wants more of you than that. What you need to do is give in! Let him have a say in your life - no longer block him out. To block out is from your human nature and is a way of holding God at arm's length so that he cannot influence you with his contagious loving kindness.miner

Of course, we need to discern the Spirit's voice when we hear it. But if it is saying things that ask you to be loving, compassionate or a builder of relationships, then you must be hearing the voice of our God who saves. The one who builds and never diminishes us. The Spirit will never ask us to break or destroy, that voice is the deceiver's voice, and the deceiver wants the opposite of what God wants.

You might say how will I know if I get it right? The answer is in the doing. If God tells you to phone a friend and listen to them for half an hour. If you obey and get it wrong, God will still honour the fact that you obeyed.

I had the honour of meeting a sweet Benedictine monk once. His name was Fr Ian Petit, and he was one of the pioneers of the Charismatic Renewal in the

Catholic Church. He was such a kind man. He was fond of reminding us that the scripture doesn't say, "listen, Lord, your servant is speaking" it says, "speak Lord your servant is listening."

We need to dare to believe that God has a purpose and a plan for our lives. That he wants more of us than what we currently give. That he will bless us when we take steps in faith. We need to dare to believe in the loving-kindness of "the heart of our God" and let it influence our actions. You can do no wrong by trying to bless another person's life if you do it with kindness and grace.

We are all fellow pilgrims on a journey into the heart of God. I pray that I can remember that. Pilgrims share the good things that they have with others on the journey and don't hide their bread from one another.

Dear Lord, let me listen to your voice. Send your Holy Spirit again to my life, renewing it and refreshing it. Let me be gentle. Amen

LIVE BY THE SPIRIT (5) - GIVE UP JUDGING

> "Do not judge others, and God will not judge you; do not condemn others, and God will not condemn you; forgive others, and God will forgive you. Give to others, and God will give to you. Indeed, you will receive a full measure, a generous helping, poured into your hands--all that you can hold. The measure you use for others is the one that God will use for you." Luke 6:37

    To live by the Spirit requires us to have a different worldview. This is because God does not see as man sees and so when we start to think like him an alternative way of seeing starts to be evident in our lives. When the Spirit comes and places his stamp of ownership on us, he inevitably brings us to a point where something happens within because the Holy Spirit is a heart changer when he enters our life. When the Spirit comes, he brings compassion for others. This initial conversion and subsequent conversions make us more loving. There are so many accounts of transformation in the lives of the Saints. John Wesley, for example, tells us how his heart was 'strangely warmed' by the Spirit empowering his ministry and changing his life. St Francis encountered God and changed radically. We change because we start to adopt God's view of others. Compassion pierces our heart, and we see our neighbour differently. When we see as God sees we see beyond what people do, to see them with some of the kind of love that God has for them.
    But after our initial Holy Spirit experience, we need in our more mundane daily lives a mechanism to keep the Spirit's life at work. And that is what we have been talking about these last few pages. Learning not to judge is an essential component part.
    Our problem is that we are prone to lose the ground that we gained previously. To give it away. One of the ways we give it away quickest is when we start to have a critical spirit about other people. Criticising others is like throwing tacks into the path of our spiritual life.
    But think about this! The person who helped you most in your life? What

were they like? I can almost guarantee that they were someone compassionate who accepted you as you are without judging. Someone who you trusted.

In our daily living, we need to think about Jesus words "The measure you use for others is the one that God will use for you."

We do all this while we are still called daily to discern between good and evil in our choices. Choosing that which gives life.

> For reflection:
>
> What measure am I using?
>
> Who am I judging and why?
>
> What is the difference between judgement and discernment?

Dear Lord, I so want to be your disciple, but I am also so fallible. Have mercy on me a sinner, see the good in me and lift me out of my pit of despair. Instead make me a new creation, called out of darkness into your wonderful light. Help me to love without reserve and to see as you see. Amen

LIVE BY THE SPIRIT (6) - FORGIVE

> "As water reflects a face, so one's life reflects the heart"
> Proverbs

It is an inevitable side effect of being human that we will hurt others and they will hurt us. Sometimes it will be deliberate, and at other times it will be the sad sideswipe of our own or their own incapacity to deal with life.

It's what we do with that hurt that can radically influence our life by the Spirit. Do we hold onto it letting it work its damages on our thinking and behaviour? Or are we going to allow ourselves to be different, allow ourselves to be people of the Kingdom?

Sometimes we want to hang onto our hurt because we get an almost masochistic pleasure feeling from turning it over in our mind. And it can be convenient to blame somebody else for what is going on in our life.

We can break that cycle of despair or oppression if we choose to. Some changes are always in our power to make. And also there is God's life-changing Holy Spirit power available in forgiveness.

Believe me; I know what I am talking about. I am the son of a chronic alcoholic, and for a long time, I held onto (in a spirit of unforgiveness) the damages he had caused to my life. But it was through listening to God's father heart and his teaching on forgiveness, that I learnt that I could surrender that hurt and let God's grace work on it and change my inner life. It was a slow process, but I have received my inner healing, and I want you to know that, if you dare, you can receive yours.

I think it is essential to the life of the Spirit to ask God who we should be forgiving and also to ask who we have offended.

Once we have his answer (our heart will also help us know who), there are two actions that we need to take. Pray hard for God's grace to change your heart, so that you are given by Jesus the desire to forgive.

When you have reached the moment. Find a wise person and discuss how you can take it forward. God might give you the desire to verbalise your forgiveness, but for it to be sincere, we have to do it with due consideration. Years or decades may have elapsed since we received the hurt or inflicted the hurt.

I urge you to let God speak to you in this whole area. Remember he is like the father in the parable of the Prodigal Son. Ready to come out on the road to welcome you back. Luke 15:11-32

I wish peace to your heart this day as God speaks to you. May you understand life can be different and that the Holy Spirit has healing powers for us. May the Spirit visit you as you think about this. Amen

LIVE BY THE SPIRIT (7) - OUR FATHER

The final message in this series takes us back to a Jesus team basic. This prayer was taught by Jesus to the twelve but also to his disciples and believers.

> Our Father, Who art in Heaven, hallowed be
> Thy Name. Thy Kingdom come. Thy Will be done,
> on earth, as it is in Heaven. Give us this day our
> daily bread and forgive us our trespasses as we
> forgive those who trespass against us; and lead us
> not into temptation, but deliver us from evil. Amen. (traditional version)

If you have been around Christians awhile, you will be aware that this prayer is part of the scenery of Church life, but each time we say it we should try our best and hear ourselves saying it for the first time. Why? Because if Jesus taught us to say it daily, it is important. The reason is that for the serious disciple it is an aide memoir to help us consistently remember the component parts of prayer. And so! Next time you say or hear it I want the words TEAM PRAYER to flash into your mind. And savour its wisdom and meaning. It is for meditation and for saying daily. Let's have a look why.

Our Father, who art in Heaven - reminds us that our life comes from God. Our dad in heaven - perfect father to us. Our dad like earthly dads is greater than us his children. Perfectly loving us (unlike our fallible earthly dads). This opening phrase reminds us where we are in the relationship. That God is greater than us. That as the author of our lives he is greater and more knowledgeable about us. We should enter prayer with that thought.

Hallowed be Thy Name - These days we would say "Holy is your name" - A reminder that there is power in God's name. As it says in the Acts of the Apostles, there is no other name by which we can be saved. As followers Jesus wants us to have that thought always before us.

Thy Kingdom come - We are here to build your Kingdom here on earth. As Kingdom builders, we yearn for it's coming fully to our neighbourhood. We will do us best to enable it! Not hinder it!

Thy Will be done, on earth, as it is in Heaven - There is no point ever, and I mean ever, praying for something that is against God's will. If we desire something illicit, we need to ask God to convert our heart. We align ourselves with his will.

Give us this day our daily bread - We ask God to provide for our needs, through our labour, daily. Notice it doesn't mention a Porsche! Just bread, asking God that we always have the daily necessaries.

Forgive us our trespasses as we forgive those who trespass against us; and lead us not into temptation – This is a reminder to live in daily repentance. Daily we have to forgive others and receive their forgiveness. Very necessary in family life. In our immediate family and beyond where would we be without this! No long-held grudges are allowed in the Christian life. If you have one lurking in your life surrender it today!

But deliver us from evil. A reminder that God is more powerful than any evil we will encounter in our daily life. Stronger than the darkness we encounter.

For meditation:

One day Jesus was praying in a certain place. When he had finished, one of his disciples said to him, "Lord, teach us to pray, just as John taught his disciples."

Jesus said to them,

"When you pray, say this:

'Father: May your holy name be honoured; may your Kingdom come.

Give us day by day the food we need.

Forgive us our sins, for we forgive everyone who does us wrong.

And do not bring us to hard testing.'"

And Jesus said to his disciples, "Suppose one of you should go to a friend's house at midnight and say, 'Friend, let me borrow three loaves of bread. A friend of mine who is on a trip has just come to my house, and I don't have any food for him!' And suppose your friend should answer from inside, 'Don't bother me! The door is already locked, and my children and I are in bed. I can't get up and give you anything.' Well, what then? I tell you that even if he will not get up and give you the bread because you are his friend, yet he will get up and give you everything you need because you are not ashamed to keep on asking. And so I say to you: Ask, and you will receive; seek, and you will find; knock, and the door will be opened to you. Luke 11:1-9 GNT

Dear Lord, open our hearts in prayer. Let your
Spirit come in to teach us! Amen

HOW AWESOME IS GOD?

> How awesome is God as he comes from his sanctuary-- the God of Israel! He gives strength and power to his people. Praise God!

That quote comes from Psalm 68, a longish triumphant song of jubilation written by David. It also has the phrase in it "Our God is a God who saves."

One of my favourite Dylan albums is Shot of Love. The title song says, "I need a shot of love, I don't need a shot of heroin to kill my disease." Yes, it's true that our disease or our uneasiness is one of the biggest problems that we face in life. We need to find a solution to that feeling. This is probably the reason that some of us get caught up in addictive behaviour. And we all do at times. St Augustine put it like this "'You have made us for yourself, O Lord, and our hearts are restless until they find their rest in you'"

I wonder if you have ever read Slaughterhouse 5 by Kurt Vonnegut? It's an amazing book. Very funny in places but also darkly addressing the question of war and how it impacts on the human heart. In it, Vonnegut gets his character Billy Pilgrim to soliloquise about religion. I haven't been able to find the exact quote, but Billy concludes that religion is a "fova" that humankind has invented to cope with life. A fova is a word that Vonnegut uses which he says means "harmless lie."

When I read the book as a young man, this really impacted me and made me question my belief in Christ. It made me ask myself was I pursuing a harmless lie? The honest answer this older version of Simon can give you is that God has proved himself too many times to me for me to doubt any more. He has changed my heart through inner healing received (forgive me if I am repeating myself), and through the trickle down of other spiritual experiences. He is a God who can answer prayers in his own unique ways. Sending you people who seem almost like angels.

Today I can honestly say I am convinced that if you turn to him, he will bless you. This is true even if you have never had a thought about God before in your life, or if you have been an intellectual Christian your entire life.

Martin Luther King used to talk about three conversions being necessary for a person's life. Conversion of heart, conversion of mind, conversion of wallet. The last one is about almsgiving I think, but the important point is, have you let God into your life at more than just an intellectual level? He wants to be in your heart's life. To perform a heart conversion on you. So that you can feel for the things that he feels for.

He wants to come into your heart and say "today I have become your father" – turn to God, of your own free will, he is a heart changer.

For reflection:
"I will hear what the Lord God has to say, a voice that speaks of peace, peace for his people and his friends, his help is near for those who fear him, and his glory will dwell in our land" Psalm 85:9 Grail Translation

Dear Lord, help me to listen to you today. Bless my life and change my thinking. Open my heart to your compassion and healing love. Amen

STAND READY

> 'Stay awake, because you do not know the day when your master is coming. You may be quite sure of this that if the householder had known at what time of the night the burglar would come, he would have stayed awake and would not have allowed anyone to break through the wall of his house. Therefore, you too must stand ready because the Son of Man is coming at an hour you do not expect. Matthew 24:42-51 JB

Stand ready then!   The invitation from Jesus is that we should not put off until tomorrow what we should be doing today. Our decision and response is invited today. Now - at this very moment we are called out of our darkness into the very presence of God our creator. The God who knows intimately what is best for us and how he can lead us into wholeness. There is no stuffiness in him just Love, pure love, for us to bathe in and receive and pass onto others.

God is calling to you just as he did to Samuel in the Old Testament. Remember Samuel did not know that it was possible to hear the voice of God. He was Eli's servant, one night he went to bed and heard the Lord's voice when he was lying down in the house of the Lord, where the ark of God was. Samuel thought it was his master, so he ran to Eli and said, "Here I am; you called me." But Eli said, "I did not call; go back and lie down." So he went and lay down. Again the Lord called, "Samuel!" And Samuel got up and went to Eli and said, "Here I am; you called me." Eli said, " My son, I did not call; go back and lie down." This continued, the third time that it happened Eli realised that in fact, it was the Lord God who was calling the boy. So Eli told Samuel, "Go and lie down, and if he calls you, say, 'Speak, Lord, for your servant is listening.'" So Samuel went and lay down in his place. The Lord came and stood there, calling as at the other times, "Samuel! Samuel!" Then Samuel said, "Speak, for your servant is listening."

Now God had Samuel's attention he says "See, I am about to do something in Israel that will make the ears of everyone who hears about it tingle."   It was through these first words that Samuel heard that God called him into the ministry of a prophet.

God seems to call people in ways that speak to them uniquely. So although he called Samuel audibly with others, he uses different methods adapting to the individual. To some, he just gives a quiet certainty. To some, he speaks to through his preachers. To some, he speaks to through nature and others through art or music.

Samuel discussed what had happened with Eli and he was guided by him with these words "He is the Lord; let him do what is good in his eyes." God's voice can only lead us to do good or loving actions. When we hear the Lord like Samuel, we need to discern what we hear.

Our difficulty in hearing God and letting him do good in our lives is that there are counterforces at work in us. These counterforces can let God's words to us fall to the ground. Sometimes we let our self-doubt and negativity speak into our lives, telling us pernicious lies, that we are no good and that we should find our fulfilment in the very things that actually kill our spirit and make it harder for us to be happy. The voice that says to us wait until tomorrow and tomorrow before you take any action. And so our time evaporates out of our life before we can respond. We can erect barriers against God at the same time as paying lip service to him. I am saying this to myself as much as I am saying this to you.

There are always areas of our life that God wants us to bring to him in honesty. When we do, he will help us to move into a more loving way of being. Seemingly step by step. But if we are to "stand ready" we need to surrender what we can of the barriers to love. God will help you to change some more!

Ask yourself about these barriers
- Money - does my need to tend and protect my money prevent me from loving?
- Power - does my need to control others remove their freedom and hinder their love?
- Sex - as a sexual being am I being loving and aware of the outcomes of my actions?
- Social Media - am I using words that build up or destroy?

There is something to be said for trying to live each day as if it was the last day on earth. If that was the case today how would you be with the above areas? Remember "stand ready" in love of the Lord. Remember "with the Lord there is mercy and fullness of redemption."

Dear Lord, forgive me for the times when I wander away from your Spirit. Help me to focus my life fruitfully on the Kingdom of God. Amen

WHAT I WANT IS LOVE NOT SACRIFICE

> "What I want is love, not sacrifice; knowledge of God, not holocausts." Hosea 6.6 Jerusalem Bible

I feel that God has brought my attention back to this message from the Prophet Hosea. His insight into the heart of God has spoken to me many times over the years. It goes to the heart of our attitude to our faith and explodes our mistaken attitudes.

Our God is a patient father and likes to teach us again the lessons that we thought we already knew. This is because there is always more to learn. Or perhaps in my case because he needs to keep me on track.

I met my friend Chris for breakfast the other morning and afterwards we went for a walk by the river. It was deliberately a prayer walk, so our chat turned to what God had been saying to him. We started looking at Matthew 9.9. Where God calls Levi (Matthew) the tax collector out of his booth and tells him to follow him. Almost immediately it seems Jesus falls to be criticised by the Pharisees for hanging around with tax collectors. This is his reply to the criticism, "People who are well do not need a doctor, but only those who are sick. Go and find out what is meant by the scripture that says: 'It is kindness that I want, not animal sacrifices.' I have not come to call respectable people, but outcasts."

Most bibles show this as a quote from Hosea 6.6. Jesus quotes it to the Pharisees because it is the bible that they have supposedly studied deeply all their lives in order to qualify as teachers- and hence they should have known it thoroughly. But sometimes we can know something and not fully put it into practice.

So I am relearning Hosea. Jesus is saying to us that when we sin we can atone for it, make things right, by making our love evident in reality. Making our love real and not just a concept. He is saying that the old religious way of atonement, burning an animal as an offering to God is not enough. God does not want burnt, charred animals from me! He wants me to practise Love. The kind of Love that is mercy and kindness.

A heart conversion is what is needed. Not just a physical action like burning an animal. A change of heart. To consciously be loving in our behaviour. To behave differently to those who we come across in our daily life. This doesn't only entail being kind and merciful to those we already love, but it goes wider to mean virtually anyone that we meet in our daily lives.

By doing this, we can participate in redemption. We can make our day better and the day of those we meet. It is better to build up rather than destroy.

Dear God, change my heart again. Remove any harshness from my daily transactions. Make me tenderhearted and prone to kindness. Refuse any "burnt offering" from me – teach me to see through your eyes and live according to your priorities. Amen

BE STILL AND KNOW THAT I AM GOD

> He says, "Be still, and know that I am God; I will be exalted among the nations, will be exalted in the earth." The Lord Almighty is with us; the God of Jacob is our fortress. Psalm 46:10-11 NIV

It has been a bit of a weird week. There has been a lot of training activity and a lot of things to absorb. At the end of my running around, I realise that mostly accidentally my quiet time has been missed.

What is interesting to me is that I can already feel that I am off kilter, slightly away from my proper path. I am a morning person, so my normal habit is to pray in the morning. For me it allows a sense of peace to enter my life. And a chance to "centre down" as some people say and listen to God and let him speak into my life. Now that I realise this I have resolved to get back on track.

Anyone who knows me knows that I am not a Saint or anything. Just an everyday sinner who has discovered that life is better when you pray. Sin separates us from God, so prayer restores us and narrows the gap between us.

As it says in the reading above "be still and know that I am God" - it might take us years to learn that fact, but learn it we should.

If today you feel ragged inside your mind, or distracted, or unhappy. I beg you turn today to your Lord and your God. Experiment at first if you like, especially if you don't believe me. Find somewhere quiet if you can. Turn your phone off or at least put it on silent. Sit there and say to God, "here I am" that's the hardest part just getting to that point. After that read a psalm or just listen. You need to experiment with what works best for you. But remember it's about slowing down and letting God speak into your life. The more you do it, the better you will feel. But it's not just about feelings. Somehow in the quietness, God comes in and instructs us and loves us.

> Then a voice said to him, "What are you doing here, Elijah?" 1 Kings 19:11-13 NIV

WATCHING FOR THE INVITATION

There have been times in my life when I haven't believed in God. But somehow God has always brought me back to himself. How this happens is through the invitation of God. He continually invites me into a relationship with him. When in my unbelief, I stumble upon one of these "invitations" I can't help but respond.

Jesus is one of these invitations. If we study his life and sayings, his behaviour. What he says and does is so extraordinary that it stands out that he is quite unlike any other prophet that ever lived. This is because when he ministers to us, it as God among us. His ministry goes beyond that of a prophet. He is Messiah, king, Son of God, teacher, revolutionary all rolled into one.

Other invitations can come from friends or family or circumstances of our life. One musician was converted when he was gazing at a painting in a church. Somehow God chose that moment to break through.

We are told in the psalms "the fool has said in his heart there is no God." This seems harsh in some ways. But I think that depends on how we think about it. My feeling is that it means that we are a fool to deprive ourselves of the good that true faith in God can bring into our lives. What good do we do ourselves to deny God a chance to speak into our life? Especially if when he does come near he brings good gifts which enrich our love.

The words of one of Jesus followers always stick in my memory as a kind of prayer of belief and praise.

Simon Peter, says to Jesus "Lord, to whom would we go? You have the words that give eternal life. And now we believe and know that you are the Holy One who has come from God." John 6:68-69 GNT

Dear Lord, I pray that I may see your invitations to me and respond. Your presence can rescue me from despair and bring me into the fullness of life.

FOLLOW THE WAY OF LOVE, THE EXAMPLE OF CHRIST WHO LOVES YOU

Some parts of the bible seem to speak to me because of their brevity and truth. It seems God's first messengers discovered a penchant for text message length 'sayings' long before we did. I think some of this is due to God's clarity in communication. He doesn't like to beat around the bush. But quite often these short sayings are really a summary of a longer teaching and meditation on them opens the mind to a whole profound and rich area of thinking.

At an evening meeting we used a reading from Ephesians 5, out of it I plucked the sentence "Follow the way of love, the example of Christ who loved you" - and have been thinking about it since.

It is a phrase that needs unpacking. What for example is the "Way of Love" that is referred to? Love, after all, is a many-faceted thing. But Gods way of love is to show his abundant love to all of humankind, and even creation. This love manifests itself as a sort of unfathomable goodwill shown to all without exception. This is because God wants the whole of creation to succeed and flourish, including you and me, and also the extremely poor as well as the rich. This demonstrates that the economy of God's world operates differently to the economy of the commercial world. Life in all its entirety is given without charge and the conditions to sustain it come readily from the world's resources. And what God requires of us in recompense for all this is that we too should be just as loving in our turn. A radical thought. That we should love in the same unconditional way that God has already loved us.

"Follow the way of love" -then can mean then that we should live our lives with the same kind of radical good will that God manifests. To have automatic care and concern for other people that is contrary to the way that the world looks at things. This is the sort of love that Jesus showed after all. How challenging that is!

The world says to charge for everything! Sell your labour and your produce for a good price. Sell your second-hand goods. But what God wants for us is subsistence in material terms and superabundance in mercy, love and kindness.

We love a God who challenges us not only to love the loveable but also to turn our efforts to love even our enemies! The way of love challenges us to have a complete heart conversion. "If you happen to see your enemy's cow or donkey running loose, take it back to him. If his donkey has fallen under its load, help him get the donkey to its feet again; don't just walk off. Exodus 23:4-5 GNB

Whereas the prophets challenge those who are rich even further, telling us not to be stingy. Amos particularly warns against over harvesting the world's resources if that means leaving nothing for the poor to pick up. In God's law, the gleanings were to be left for the poor.

The way of love requires us to hear the cry of the poor. To no longer live in the hardness of heart that makes us deaf to their appeals.

Dear Jesus, you called me out my darkness. I have been tempted to continue walking in the dark. I have fooled myself into thinking it was easy for you because you are the Son of God. But now I see how completely you surrendered to the will of the father. Call me out of the darkness of my selfishness into your wonderful light. Give me an experience of your love so that I may share it to the ends of the earth. My brother, my saviour Amen

"Let the one who walks in the dark, who has no light, trust in the name of the LORD." Isaiah 50:10-11

LET THE SPIRIT DIRECT YOUR LIVES

> May the words of my mouth and the meditations of my heart find favour in your sight, O Lord - my redeemer, my rock!
> Psalm 20:15

The above is a good prayer to start a prayer time with or even to use as just a short plea to God asking him to guide our day. After all what we say and think are precursors to our actions.

My perception is that my days are better if I have made time to think and pray in the morning. The truth be known it might even make me better tempered!

St Paul advises us to "Let the Spirit direct your lives" (Galatians 5:16) and if we are going to do that we need to find the time to let that happen. We so easily fritter our lives away watching adverts or waiting for computers to boot up or gazing at the back of a cereal packet. All things we have chosen to do in a way albeit unconsciously perhaps. Can we find a little time for God in the midst of this?

But if we take St Paul's words seriously, the Holy Spirit should be what gives our lives strategic direction. And listening for its guidance should be what makes our Christian life move into a more authentic level of being.

In this life when we have so many choices, may one of them be to try and listen to the Spirit. I can promise that doing this will change your life, lifting it to a different level. Letting God's love break in.

There are plenty of examples in the news of what happens when people make decisions without listening to the Holy Spirit. It's easy to look at the extreme examples of violence and hateful behaviour and say it's clear that whatever they were listening to it wasn't the voice of God. Inevitably too there are cases of so-called religious people doing hateful things. Let's make it clear that kind of action is from the deceiver and is the opposite of what God wants.

To listen to the Spirit is to listen to the voice of God who is love. He will inspire us to walk joyfully in his peace, to love as he does.

Dear Lord, help me to see that your Spirit is for me!

GUIDE US, LORD!

> "Not by might, nor by power, but by My Spirit says the Lord of Hosts" Zechariah 4.6.

These words are from the prophet Zerubbabel and have always spoken to my heart. I find them useful as an "arrow" prayer to say at various times. Especially before meetings that look as if they have the potential to be stressful and conflicted. We need to keep on track and not be blown around chaotically by our human desires. The words remind me of what God wants.

It seems I have had various conversations about this very thing. How to keep on track! I have a problem in that I know what God wants from me I just need to find my way through to the delivery of his vision. It is my human fallibility that can get in the way. The prayer reminds me to put God's way of thinking first. To seek not my own objectives but to look for what God wants. His agenda is so often different to ours. It reminds me that the Glory must go to God and that we don't need to strive to achieve that. In fact, if we find ourselves striving then we can ask are we seeking God correctly? God has been sustaining the universe for all these thousands of years without me being number one, or head honcho! But what we can bring to situations is our genuine desire to seek God's will and to support it. Are we seeking the right sort of power in our life? I don't need to be first to speak or last to speak. Although God does want me to speak if I can contribute something to the meeting.

Although it was "meetings" that started me thinking - "Not by might, nor by power, but by My Spirit" applies to all parts of our life. Do we make bringing God's spirit a priority in our life, or do we wake in the morning to play with our gadgets, to plot our finances with the Financial Times? Or to feed our News habit? Or to plan our retirement? Maybe? But although those things might have some place. God first, our loved ones next is how we should prioritise. Then things will fall into place, and we will find a more grace-filled living experience.

If we "seek first the kingdom of God" we are putting the Spirit first. In prayer also, I heard God's voice in Galatians 5. At verse 16 he says, "What I say is this: let the Spirit direct your lives, and you will not satisfy the desires of the human nature." - One commentary I read points out that if we focus on the Spirit, God's love and Holy Spirit helps us to push out the sin in our life. The sin is displaced by the presence of the Spirit. I feel God is saying have more of the Spirit, and you will naturally become less sinful.   That means we need to worry less about our besetting sin and let go of it and run straight towards our God who is love. He will give us his love, joy and peace which can't fail to change us.

Dear Lord, help me to have more of you in my life. I seek you, Lord, show me your face. Amen

THE PLAN FOR YOUR LIFE

The truth is that God has a plan and a purpose that is unique to each one of us. God, our creator, doesn't want us all to be the same. He calls each one of us daily "out of darkness into his wonderful light." He wants us to be the best version of yourself that we can possibly manage. It might be very hard to believe that today. But take it on your heart.

On my Facebook profile is one of my favourite quotes from St Catherine of Siena, "Be who God meant you to be and you will set the world on fire."

No matter whether your situation is desperate or wonderful. God wants to be able to speak into your life and guide you. No matter what you have done God has a rescuing plan for you to pluck you out of disaster or even from mediocrity.

The first step is to have the strength, or perhaps help from someone, to believe that God is your Redeemer.

The next three steps are crucial
- Listen to your life
- Listen to what God has to say about your life
- Take action to change

In the next three entries, I will write more on each of those above subjects.

Meanwhile, for reflection, I will briefly share what is going on with me. God can be quite insistent on speaking sometimes. When I was preparing to write this, he gave me a very vivid dream about a fire, and in the dream, the reading I was given was Jeremiah 4. It wasn't a passage that I was familiar with, so I went and looked it up. Here is an excerpt from it.

> Circumcise yourselves to the Lord, circumcise your hearts, you people of Judah and inhabitants of Jerusalem, or my wrath will flare up and burn like fire because of the evil you have done-- burn with no one to quench it. Jerusalem, wash the evil from your heart and be saved. How long will you harbour wicked thoughts? Jeremiah 4:4

Just to share with you, I feel God is saying to me "put sin under lock", and then you will be able to move into the next phase in your life. That quote is from

Daniel 10:21. God says "I have come to teach it to you because God loves you. Pay attention to this word and understand the vision."

    I know from past experience if I listen to him - he will change my life

Dear Lord, I sense you want to move us into a new awareness of your love for us all. Help me to hear you and respond and not block you.

THE PLAN FOR YOUR LIFE (2) - LISTEN

> Amos 5.14 Seek good, not evil, that you may live. Then the LORD God Almighty will be with you, just as you say he is. Hate evil, love good; maintain justice in the courts.

Previously I talked about the plan for your life. I said that the first stage of finding the plan for your life is to Listen to it. By that, I mean to pause and ask yourself "what are the events and circumstances of my life saying to me?"

By doing this, we introduce to ourselves a habit of self-knowledge. It could be that you keep a journal and are already doing this to a point. But you can take things one step further and ask "Did I seek good today?" - It can be a revealing question. If we didn't seek good just how harmful have our actions been?

The reason people change when they encounter God is that he has a disconcerting tendency to hold a mirror up to our lives - so that we can see ourselves as others do. Sometimes we need to do that to recognise what is wrong with us as well as what is right with us. The mirror is there so that we can have enough self-knowledge to want to change.

If we are struggling with addiction, we can find that we haven't "sought good" because we are so busy looking to feed the addiction. It pushes our time for others out of the way.

But remember that the love that comes from God is a free gift for your life. You can exercise your own will as to whether to accept it. Let God in, and he will bring you to an exciting new phase of your life.

There is a prayer that has helped a lot of people over the years.

God grant me the serenity to accept the things I cannot change, courage to change the things I can, and the wisdom to know the difference.

JESUS FOR REAL

> "I tell you the truth, when you were younger you dressed yourself and went where you wanted; but when you are old you will stretch out your hands, and someone else will dress you and lead you where you do not want to go." John 21:18

When we are young, we understand Jesus in a very different way to the way adults understand him. Part of this is a conscious decision by adults only to tell the softer stories to their children about Jesus. But it does mean that a lot of children grow into adults with a saccharine image of "gentle" Jesus "meek and mild" wafting around that is nowhere near the character of the real Jesus. I can understand why it happens. As adults, we sometimes decide to package information differently that we deem is too hard for children to understand.

What set me thinking about this was remembering an email that my cousin had sent me about the Little   Plastic Jesus. She has given me permission to quote her.

> "I was 4, I remember walking into a large room, it was dark, it had old dark furniture, and it felt like stepping back in time! In the centre of the dark room behind a huge dark desk was a tiny old lady dressed in black. I remember thinking she looked so, so old with the wrinkliest face I had ever seen, but It was a kind face. I wonder whether I remember this in detail because my mum was probably going through the formalities of me joining the school and I had a chance just to stare! Sally, my sister, had been at the school previously, there seemed to be no issue with a Non-Catholic family sending their children to Manor House convent. My place was pretty much guaranteed.

"Mother superior chatted to me, and I can't remember what about but as we made to leave she gave me a gift- a little plastic Jesus in a little plastic manger. The little plastic manger didn't last long, it had flimsy legs and soon disintegrated. After a while, Little plastic Jesus got put in the drawers under my bed with all my other toys. Like most children, the drawers under my bed soon became filled with broken toys, toys that had been grown out of, art projects from school, old plasticine and crayons!

"Mum insisted that the drawers under my bed were subject to periodical sort-outs, I would pick up Plastic baby Jesus, invariably found hiding in the far back corner amongst the plasticine and crayons, I would pick him up, and he would get the same mental wrestling each previous item had received. 'Live another day or be relegated to the rubbish pile' Every time I had a strong feeling, ' I can't throw away baby Jesus!'

"The thing I find most amazing is the clarity in which I remember being given the gift of plastic baby Jesus -   I also find it amazing that he carried on to survive in the backs of drawers until I was 31 when I became a Christian.
" I know recently. I have been putting Jesus into a back drawer. Little plastic Jesus is a good analogy. That's why I wanted to share the story with you. But it has also made me think how I have been chosen by God and how amazingly patient he is waiting for the right time for us to grow. I don't think I could ever throw little plastic Jesus away; I couldn't throw Jesus away. But I was in great danger of relegating him to the back of a drawer."

What strikes me is that my cousin's story illustrates what happens to so many of us. We have to find a point in our lives where we discover that the Plastic Jesus of our childhood is not the only way of thinking about Jesus. That the real Jesus is waiting for us to see him as he is. Son of God, fully human and yet fully divine. Revolutionary, itinerant, prophet, teacher, rabbi, friend, wonderful counsellor, lover, challenger, penniless and homeless. This Jesus challenges us to grow from believer to disciple. This real Jesus we can discover and encounter in the Gospels but also in our daily prayer life and the sharing of so many people.

Is the Jesus you know the childhood safe one? Or is it the real Jesus who invites you to be his follower and disciple? Moving out of your comfort zone to travel with him to where you know not. He is the one who challenges us to live a spiritual life in addition to the material life, thinking beyond what's next to buy in Ikea and other shops!

This Jesus is the one who loves you and wants you to discover him. To stay in a relationship with him.

Dear Jesus, may I fully discover you! Send your wisdom and love into my life. I need it so much.
Amen

LISTEN TO WHAT GOD HAS TO SAY ABOUT YOUR LIFE

> Isaiah 55:1-3 NIV
>
> "Come, all you who are thirsty,
> come to the waters;
> and you who have no money,
> come, buy and eat!
> Come, buy wine and milk
> without money and without cost. Why spend money on what is not bread,
> and your labour on what does not satisfy?
> Listen, listen to me, and eat what is good,
> and you will delight in the richest of fare. Give ear and come to me;
> listen, that you may live.
> I will make an everlasting covenant with you,
> my faithful love promised to David.

Our rebellious side might say why listen to God? For me, the reason is that he can speak objective truth into our situation. What God says is a truth for all time and not a temporary fix. His universe is up and running, and the laws that apply will continue to apply. Our God is both amazing and perplexing in that way.

The objective truth is still there for us even when circumstances change. To witness from my own life for example. Three weeks ago, when I started this mini-series on God's Plan, I kind of knew which way I was going. Yet the circumstances of my life have changed since then. We have an issue with Debs visa to overcome and have temporarily dropped to one income. Now that all stems from a miscommunication somewhere along the line and needs to be sorted out. We are praying and listening for an answer but holding on to the objective truth that as husband and wife we need to live together. It might knock our faith a little but increases it when we come out the other side with a God blessed solution.

God's plan is the plan for your life but uniquely configured for you in version 1 which involves you and him! You need to align yourself with his personal plan for you. It uses all your strengths and can cover your weaknesses.

Yet when we go wrong, he can and does bring us back on track when we turn back to him.

God's only law is love. That law governs the whole of creation and God himself. To love is to be a part of that. The personal bit comes out of how we exercise our free will to discover how and where to love and, of course, who to love.

Because we have this free will each one of us also has the exciting prospect of discovering what our God-given talents are and then stepping out in faith and using them.

We need to concentrate always on finding the most loving solution to our opportunities and our problems. That way we cause the least collateral damage while achieving the most personal growth.

Listening to God is done through living in his words in the Bible, with the help of those who can interpret and pray them with us.

Dear Lord, reveal your path for my life. Help me to walk your path in a way that is loving and unique for me. Amen

TAKE ACTION TO CHANGE

This is the last in the miniseries "God has a plan for your life" - so it isn't about change for change's sake. It is about changing to be the best version of ourselves that we can be. To do this, we need to align our heart with what love requires of us and then take action to try and achieve that. The thing is we are never going to be perfect. But it is better to try to change rather than to think we can stand still. Because the human reality is that we never stand still, we are always changing either for better or for worse. The Dylan song puts it "he who isn't busy being born is busy dying."

So, we want to be born anew and know that change is scary for the human heart. Yet we need to put fear aside and realise that when we pray we are entering a spiritual dynamic that inevitably changes us.

So! Here is the checklist. Like driving a car some things just need to happen before we proceed.

The key in the ignition is daily prayer and Scripture reading. Allocate some time for this. It doesn't have to be a huge amount of time. Persistence is more important than quantity.

Turning the key gets the engine on. This is the exciting bit - movement is imminent. You are listening to what God and your life is saying to you.

When you reach the point where you want to go forward, you need to put your foot on the accelerator. God has shown you what you need to do. Perhaps it is who to forgive, who to ask for help, perhaps what you need to give up. You are moving forward in the knowledge that God is with you.

Be bold - take that step

Dear Lord, we rely on your mercy, bless our lives with your abundant love, let us fully comprehend it. To know you is to know the beginnings of joy in our life. Amen

"GOD WITH US" AND "GOD AMONG THE POOR"

We celebrate the birth of the Christ child. "God With Us" who was born into the humble surroundings of a stable. He dwelt amongst us in grace and truth. Living simply and in solidarity, with the poor, he taught us about God and the love that God has for each one of us.

So "God with us" and "God among the poor" is what I have been thinking about over Christmas. I felt God prompting me to think again about how radical God is in his deep love for humanity. But how God placed Jesus in quite a simple lifestyle. He was birthed into a worker's family, not into some cushy number.

I feel maybe God is also making the point that all we need for our lives is actually a sufficiency to supply our food, clothing and shelter - our true wealth is not in palaces but in our love for family, friends and of course God our saviour.

At the start of his ministry in Luke's tells us that Jesus uses words of the prophet Isaiah to announce his purpose, he read out to those in the synagogue "The Spirit of the Lord is upon me because he has anointed me to bring good news to the poor. He has sent me to proclaim release to the captives and recovery of sight to the blind, to let the oppressed go free, to proclaim the year of the Lord's favour." (Luke 4:17-21) and then said, "Today this scripture is fulfilled in your hearing."

It seems to me that if we are to have a share in his ministry we also need to bring Good News to the poor.

Jesus exercised what some Christians now call a "preferential option for the poor". I need to recognise that when I serve the poor I am responding to a call that comes from God and so in doing so you serve Jesus himself. This may sound strange, so I suggest that to try and understand further you meditate on the following:

"I tell you, indeed whenever you did this for one of the least important of these brothers of mine you did it for me!"(Matthew 25:40). The longer passage can be found between verses 31 and 40.

A quote from St. Augustine "God does not demand much of you. He asks back what he gave you, and from him, you take what is enough for you. The superfluities of the rich are the necessities of the poor. When you possess superfluities, you possess what belongs to others." from an Exposition on Psalm 147:12.

*Dear Lord, help me to find my riches in my relationships and to be generous to those in need.
Amen*

AMOS

I have been spending a bit of time with the prophet Amos lately. A prophet who could, in many ways, be speaking to our generation. A while back I took one of his passages and rewrote it into modern equivalents.

"Listen to this you who trample the needy and try to suppress the poor people of the world, you who say next month we will make a fast buck on the stock exchange. With insider dealing we will buy low and sell high, swindling the shareholders and the market. Also at the same time, we can exploit the world labour market and pay pitifully low wages to people from another country who make shoes for us and then sell them here for seventy quid. If we are smart, we can even sell the off - cuts to the fools. But Amos says I will swear by the pride of Jacob. God will not forget anything that you do!"

He challenges me to think again about God's attitude towards the poor. The Psalm very clearly says "the Lord hears the cry of the poor, blessed be his name."

The Pharisee within us might say that the poor are always with us. And use that as a comfort blanket so that we do nothing. But God's love should break through that and challenge us to "hunger and thirst for justice" and to be an advocate for the poor, who are unable to pay for their own food let alone their own advocate.

In modern Britain, the politicians are quietly busy dismantling the work of the social reformers. Some of this might be justified. After all, we have books to balance and bankers to satisfy. But we need to be careful that we don't make it all a money equation. The soul of the country needs to be invested in too. What is Britain known for these days? In our gentleman's clubs are we known only as "heroes of the wine bottle" - should we be better than this?

It seems that more of the poor sleep on our streets in modern Britain. Is that how we want to be known?

Dear Lord, help me to realise the harvest that my own actions will have on other people. Call me away from being insular and into a love relationship with God. Sow the seeds of peace in my life. Amen.

CAN THE HOLY SPIRIT MOVE YOU?

I wonder did anyone see the discussion of this on The Big Questions on BBC1 one January? It was good to see a friend Michelle Moran there on the telly with two other Christians with experience. They were all from different Christian backgrounds, but the one and same Spirit of God had moved them.

It was an interesting and thought-provoking discussion but annoying because participants are never allowed to finish their points. This comment applies to both sides! If there are sides on a question about truth like this.

To me, it is a spiritual reality or spiritual dynamic that God will allow his Holy Spirit to "move" you. In fact, much of the motive power of the Christian church comes from the working of the Spirit. It is the author of all healing and the secret ingredient of all evangelisation. The inspirer of the ordinary person just as much as the prophets, evangelists, teachers, servants "of the Lord" - also the same Spirit must I think have inspired the various Jewish Old Testament authors. Breathing God's truth into scripture.

- It inspired King David's dance of praise when his Mrs told him off.
- Moses got the ten commandments through listening to God's grace.
- Paul wrote the chapter on love (1 Corinthians 13) under the influence.
- Pentecost day itself!

Oh my! Thank you, God, for sending your Holy Spirit daily into our lives. Thank you for your loving kindness, so great, so lovely, so tender, so heartwarming. Thank you for changing my heart from stone to flesh through the Holy Spirit. This same Holy Spirit can be renewed in your life for the asking. When we call on the Lord times of spiritual strength are possible. Equipping us for our daily lives.

> *John 14:15-17, "If you love me, you will obey my commandments. I will ask the Father, and he will give you another Helper, who will stay with you forever. He is the Spirit, who reveals the truth about God. The world cannot receive him, because it cannot see him or know him. But you know him, because he remains with you and is in you.*

THE BIRD FEEDER

I was sitting yesterday eating my breakfast and watching the birds coming to the bird feeder. It was quite funny to watch their behaviour. The younger or smaller birds won't feed while the bigger ones are around. Although they might try a quick and sneaky peck while the bigger bird isn't facing them. Even the bigger birds have their own order. The female blackbird gives way to her mate. If the collared doves are around all the other birds vanish. I don't know if this behaviour is learnt by the birds or whether it is instinctive. So far I haven't noticed birds pecking each other at the feeder. The suet treats and other beneficence come from Debs, and she is happy for any birds that want to, just to help themselves.

My thoughts then drifted off into human life. I was thinking that sometimes I hold back from doing things because someone I perceive as better than me is around and I think they should go first as they are better. Sometimes I hold back because of the throng. In families, there can be a definite feeding order. And the youngest can be fed first. My friend Veronica told me that at parties sometimes when the food might not be enough, the word might go out from her mum "family hold back" – that meant the visitors had to be allowed to grab the grub first.

In God's Kingdom, things work differently in my experience. Everything is available for everyone. God has no favourites, and his abundant blessing is available in full measure to whoever wants to come to the feeder. No one is better than anyone else. All welcome! We need to turn off our inner voice that says someone better than me should go first. And to understand that in Christ Jesus we are all made worthy. Our inheritance is there waiting for us as soon as we realise it.

Dear Lord, help me to accept your invitation for my life to be transformed. Amen

40 YEARS, 40 DAYS OR 40 SECONDS?

I have an Android phone, and if I download an App for it, I am happy if it downloads in forty seconds. My expectation is set at that level by modern technology. In the early days of computing our expectations were much lower. It could take hours to download new software, and even then it could sometimes crash, and the whole process would have to be started again. The expectation nowadays is instant results. But it is not that long ago that we had to work harder at all things. I remember hearing on the TV, on "Who Do You Think You Are?" About a couple whose relationship had started as pen friends during the war. They exchanged a letter a week with each other, and some of the letters even got lost between the war front and home. Their friendship and love had to blossom into romance and eventual marriage with these inevitable gaps in between hearing from each other. I am not sure we could easily do that nowadays. But if something is good it is worth waiting for, isn't it? The experience of waiting can promote a greater degree of understanding.

Now we are all probably in either a love or hate relationship with God. I have met very few people who are genuinely indifferent towards him.

He is an amazing God it is true, yet at the same time enigmatic and elusive. A God of mystery who sometimes makes himself very clear. Sometimes we just don't get him however hard we try. Some spiritual writers talk about a Dark Night of the Soul which can last for years, where they cling almost to their belief and memories of a merciful God, like those two lovers clutching their photographs, waiting for him to speak again.

Moses spent forty years as a shepherd before God spoke to him and called him. Maybe he needed that time to prepare himself to be open enough for the task that God had assigned to him. Or maybe it took forty years to develop the ability to hear the Lord.

Jesus spent forty days in the desert before he began his ministry. During the forty days, the devil tried to distract him from starting his ministry by tempting him. The desert became a war zone between Jesus and temptation.

It seems that God sends us love letters all our life, sometimes they get intercepted between the war front and home and so we never get to open them or understand them. The ones we open - we sometimes understand and appreciate. Sometimes we write back and have enthusiasm in our hearts for a few days. Other times we think "that's nice" and put them to one side thinking we will reply later.

God is the "gentle invader" of our life. Seeking always to start a relationship with us, without forcing the issue. Because for love to be real it needs to be freely given and not forced. Sometimes we just can't see who or what is good for us. God is good for us! He heals us and makes us whole. He invites us constantly, but our intentions and our hearts go astray, and we can't answer. But still, he calls us into a relationship.

I realise I have spent a lot of my life blowing hot and cold for the Lord. But that has changed. I am seeking his face, his love in my life, his healing, his plan. Because I have discovered in my detours that, in fact, he is the ultimate good that I need.

No compromises any more, my yes will be yes, my heart is being converted – will you allow Jesus to break through your defences? Jesus, may I be a man after your own heart. But it will take more than forty seconds. Possibly more than forty days. But if I listen, it will be less. You, at last, have my attention, Lord. Teach me to listen.

> But as surely as God is faithful, our message to you is not "Yes" and "No." For the Son of God, Jesus Christ, who was preached among you by us--by me and Silas and Timothy--was not "Yes" and "No," but in him it has always been "Yes." For no matter how many promises God has made, they are "Yes" in Christ. And so through him the "Amen" is spoken by us to the glory of God. Now it is God who makes both us and you stand firm in Christ. He anointed us, set his seal of ownership on us, and put his Spirit in our hearts as a deposit, guaranteeing what is to come. 2 Corinthians 1:18-22 NIV

Dear Jesus, I want more of you in my life. Help me to let you in. Keep fear out and let me know the love of God in a new way that makes me more compassionate. Amen

REMEMBER THE ROCK FROM WHICH YOU ARE HEWN

> "Love must be completely sincere. Hate what is evil, hold on to what is good." Romans 12:9 GNT

and

> "Listen to me, you who pursue righteousness and who seek the Lord: Look to the rock from which you were cut and to the quarry from which you were hewn" Isaiah 51:1 NIV

I think these days we are hungry for authenticity. So much about our culture and politics is so fake and superficial that we long for the genuine version of something. We want people we can trust around us. People who "get us" and don't undermine us. I think the first passage is a call to arms to remind us that if we want this from other people, we need to be like that ourselves. It's no good expecting one standard from them and being flakey ourselves.

The word itself "Love" is elusive in meaning. When we use it, it can have four or five shades of meaning, But for our love to flourish, as it is meant to, God wants it to be deeply anchored in what is good. We need therefore to keep him in sight trying to let his love rule our lives and our behaviours.

It isn't easy, and we must be realistic about it and acknowledge that every now and then we will fail and people we know quite well will also fail. By holding onto "the good" we see beyond our failures and acknowledge that the human heart is born to be noble. The good in people mostly outweighs the evil they do. As it says in the gospel of John "the light is stronger than the darkness."

Of course, sin by its nature is wrong. We are however called by Christ to love the person who sins. We can love them without condoning or "agreeing" to their sin. St Thomas Aquinas says - "To Love is to will the good of another" - to keep treating people with goodwill in difficult or perplexing circumstances is a sign of God's kingdom of love being built in us.

To give us the strength to do this we look to the rock from which we are hewn. We are cut from the rock of God, the sure rock who saves us! A rock that is steadfast and in whose cleft we can shelter when the storm comes. Not a crumbly rock! Because it is good quality rock that we come from it can take a while to quarry us. God is a rock of love, from which more love can be quarried.

Dear Lord, strengthen and purify my love. Lead me into your kingdom of love. Let me be real with people, wholehearted, sincere, loving and teach me how to eject evil from my life! Amen

MY LORD AND MY GOD

> Thomas said to Jesus, "My Lord and my God!" Jesus replied, "You believe because you can see me. Blessed are those who have not seen and yet believe." (John 20:24-29)

The full version of this passage has some very strong messages in it and can be a turning point for us in our understanding of Jesus. Thomas actually put his finger into the wounds of Jesus. This quelled his doubt. Just before this Jesus had said to him 'Peace be with you' and then 'Put your finger here; look, here are my hands. Give me your hand; put it into my side. Doubt no longer but believe.'

It emphasises for us that there has been a physical resurrection, that Jesus literally got up after being dead and that he walked about. Something seemingly impossible for someone who had been wounded and killed so thoroughly, but to God everything is possible.

To help us believe this, we have the witness statements of those that saw him. For example, John the author of this passage is one of the disciples that met the risen Lord. We can say as St Paul says in one of his letters: "We don't rely on made up stories" and it is evident that he made close enquiry into this when he first became a Christian as he says elsewhere "I passed on to you what I received, which is of the greatest importance: that Christ died for our sins, as written in the scriptures; that he was buried, that he was raised to life three days later, as written in the scriptures; that he appeared to Peter and then to all twelve apostles. Then he appeared to more than five hundred of his followers at once, most of whom are still alive, although some have died. Then he appeared to James, and afterwards to all the apostles." Paul knew most of these people, and his summary is the result of careful enquiry.

The resurrection is the essential proof that Jesus is the Son of God. If there is no resurrection, there could still be doubt. We might say as the centurion did that "Jesus was a good man", but because Jesus rose from the dead we can go far beyond this and say Jesus is the Son of God that only God could snatch victory from the closing jaws of sin and death.

The reading also speaks powerfully about the suffering of Jesus. As any nurse will tell you there is great intimacy in touching the wounds of another. It excites compassion in the most stony-hearted of us. Thomas must have felt that in touching the wounds of Jesus. We can also imagine with some certainty that Thomas was dissolved as he saw at close sight what Jesus had gone through. No wonder Thomas then said to Jesus "My Lord and my God."

What is important to remember also today is that Jesus gives the disciples the Holy Spirit. The Holy Spirit transforms them from fearful timidity, after all, they had been described as "cowering," into people who can boldly share their faith. The Christian faith is about people whose lives can be transformed. When invited God's Holy Spirit comes into our life - He stands by us as our advocate and strengthener.

I pray today for all readers of this, wherever we are in our faith may we be strengthened by what we have read, let us be inspired by Thomas words and say to Jesus "My Lord and my God."

AVOIDING THE DRAGNET OF EVIL

Put at its starkest level sometimes Christianity is about the struggle between good and evil. The struggle between love and hate. And the choice between what helps us and that which harms us.

What has provoked those thoughts in me is rather randomly last Thursday I put my toe in the water of the book of Habakkuk. The same day I started to read Christine Caine's book Undaunted. Both books gripped me and started me thinking along the same lines.

To be a follower of Christ rather than just a believer means that we are called to an active opposition of evil. You could term it spiritual opposition, but it can also be said that we are called to a direct opposition of evil where it is manifest in our world. Bear with me please and follow me to where I go with this.

First Habakkuk. I put my toe in the book thinking I was just going to read a passage but had to read the whole of the short book to try and understand it. I found myself thinking about a description that the prophet uses, "dragnet of evil, " he warns us that we are like fishes in the sea and that we can be unwittingly caught up in that dragnet of evil. Sucked into evil without at first being aware of what is happening. The dragnet can plunge towards us, and before we know it, we can be deep in the net with our tail flicking in panic.

I have come to realise that the main times that this happens is when we come into contact with the off-shoots of organised crime or institutional and corporate sin.

We have to allow the scales to fall off our eyes and to be aware that these "dragnets" reach our local communities. Our first response should be to say "no" to their products ourselves and teach our children to. That's a definite no to soft drugs, money lending, counterfeit goods, heroin, pimps, pornography. If they can't sell their products, they lose the incentive to be in your neighbourhood. All these products are produced through coercion in some way and to deliver the product a human has suffered. Even if the first fix was free.

The link to Christine Caine's book Undaunted is that she brings, as her witness to us, a meeting that she had with some young women who had escaped human trafficking. The account is very moving and should be of concern to us. She explains why she started the A21 campaign in 2007.

Does the dragnet of evil come near to me or someone I care about?

Your eyes are too pure to look on evil; you cannot tolerate wrongdoing. Why then do you tolerate the treacherous? Why are you silent while the wicked swallow up those more righteous than themselves? You have made people like the fish in the sea, like the sea creatures that have no ruler. The wicked foe pulls all of them up with hooks, he catches them in his net, he gathers them up in his dragnet; and so he rejoices and is glad. Therefore he sacrifices to his net and burns incense to his dragnet, for by his net he lives in luxury and enjoys the choicest food. Is he to keep on emptying his net, destroying nations without mercy? Habakkuk 1:13-17 NIV

Do I passively accept evil? Gulp!

Be under obligation to no one--the only obligation you have is to love one another. Whoever does this has obeyed the Law. The commandments, "Do not commit adultery; do not commit murder; do not steal; do not desire what belongs to someone else"--all these, and any others besides, are summed up in the one command, "Love your neighbour as you love yourself." If you love others, you will never do them wrong; to love, then, is to obey the whole Law. Romans 13:8-10 GNT

Dear Lord, open my eyes. Purify my heart and my intentions, free me from pressure to do things I don't want to do. I want to freely dedicate myself to seeking your peace and your love for my life.
Amen

THE POOR

> Looking at his disciples, he said: "Blessed are you who are poor, for yours is the kingdom of God.

Here was a man whose words were like fire.

Even now Jesus words can penetrate our comfortable world and challenge us so that we can dare to be different.

Here is a man who presents to us an altered perception of what it means to be living the human life. Here is a man whose words can make us question our existing value system and drag us out of our introspection.

Jesus trades in paradox. We start to listen to him and when we hear him say "BLESSED," "POOR,""KINGDOM OF GOD" in the same sentence we begin to question what he could possibly mean.

The Good News translation even says "Happy" instead of "Blessed "How can poor people be happy? How can the hungry be satisfied? In a way, the beatitudes are one of the most frightening passages that Jesus teaches. Because what he says invades our life. We spend most of our lives working hard to feed our family, clothe them, pay a mortgage, buy a car (and of course be a success in the process) and yet Jesus comes close to us in today's gospel and says, "alas for you who are rich: you are having your consolation now."

It is not something that we should explain away or dilute. Jesus words are addressed to us all at an individual level. To each one who listens they are a challenge. They are a challenge to our hearts and directly to our interior lives. Jesus is prompting us in a very direct way to change the orientation of our lives so that we put the God who Is Love first and everything else second. He is inviting us to have spiritual integrity, and part of having this is to be able to detach from material possessions so that they no longer own us.

You could also say that Jesus words are addressed to us so that we change our hearts from stone to compassionate hearts of flesh. This invitation is from a Jesus who wants to usher in the new reign of God. A lot of the teaching in the gospel of Luke is about the "Kingdom of God" and how to bring it into our lives. Jesus expects his followers to be "yeast" in society, to have integrity. Changing society by their very presence. If our hearts are in the right place, then this starts to happen.

Christians are not called to be passive. If our faith does anything for us at all, it should stir us into a purer kind of love which isn't at all selfish.

And yes, then the beatitudes start to come true. We are happy (or happier) when we change and live by the gospel.

Of course, we are only human and will struggle with temptation and even fall back at times. But what we need to watch is that the direction of our lives is going the right way. That is towards God and towards each other and not the other way. We need to set our rudder straight. Set our love straight. Set our integrity straight and head for the goal. Then rich or poor becomes irrelevant. I remember a good friend reminding me that we pray daily for our food in the Lord's prayer "give us this day our daily bread."

Dear Jesus, I hold so much, please help me to know this and still to live fully as an heir to the kingdom.
Amen

COLLISION COURSE

Our bird feeder is quite near the side of our house. We have been visited daily by a little chaffinch who has been visiting the feeder. At 6am yesterday, bless him, he took again to his favourite activity of dive bombing our Windows. He is the only bird doing it, and we have got so used to him doing it that we know that the tap, tap, tap sound is him again and so sometimes will lurch out of bed to look at him. So we have learnt from his behaviour. He, however, has learnt nothing from these collisions beak first with our double glazing. They must be painful for his little beak.

This has been going on in my week of listening to God about the future. It made me think have there been times in my life where I have been like that chaffinch. Repeating behaviours or actions without drawing any conclusion as to whether they were good for me, even though sometimes they hurt more than banging a beak against glass!! I think, to be truthful, yes at times I have been like that chaffinch. So that set me thinking on the whole area of how do I live my life?

At a logical level, it makes sense to humanly concentrate on the things that build me up or fulfil me.

There is a quote in the book Birdsong by Sebastian Faulks which captures what we sometimes realise - "There's nothing more than to love and be loved."

To me to give and receive love is what makes the difference between a life well lived and one of despair. And that to have love in my life enriches my Spirit.

It may not be fashionable to acknowledge it, but we are also spiritual creatures. We have our bodies and our mind, and we have a spiritual life which needs nourishment too.

I choose life, and I choose love, I choose to trust the creator - I hope you can too. I invite you to discover something that gives me strength.

MARSH WARBLER

Let me tell you about the Marsh Warbler. John and I were on one of our birding trips, and we were going down one of the less trodden paths on the reserve. Something made us stop and take note. From one bush was coming all this birdsong. A seemingly impossible amount of birds in the reed bed. It took us a while to understand what was going on. One bird, a little Marsh Warbler, was mimicking the voice of other birds. John counted that it was imitating eight other identifiable bird songs as well as his own. But amongst this amazingly there was an unidentifiable song too. Possibly from Africa.

We were on this spot for about an hour and a half. Listening and enjoying the performance but also trying to see the bird itself. We were finding it impossible to get a clear view of this rare little fellow. Eventually, in desperation, I said a little prayer along the lines of "I don't deserve this Lord, but please let us see him" - shortly after a chaffinch came in and dive-bombed the Marsh Warbler and it broke cover and sat on a branch for a short while singing his heart out. Enough time for us to confirm identification. Then he disappeared. Great joy!

On the way home, we were chatting. We were saying persistence and patience had paid off. We were on that spot for quite a while, at least an hour and a half, and got passed by a few other birders. Me being me said to John, prayer is like that. We sometimes give in too quickly. We don't spend enough time waiting for the Lord to show himself like that. It's true we need persistence and patience in prayer too. And humility is a factor, honest humility. God is good, bigger and better than us. When we acknowledge him as a father, he will bless us.

The other thing that struck me is, like the Marsh Warbler we disguise our real voices sometimes. Maybe to hide or to protect ourselves, but we should really allow our real voice to be heard. I wanted to hear the real song of the Marsh Warbler too. I am not sure I ever did. God wants our real voice in prayer. We need to be vulnerable to God. It is Yahweh who is to be the subject of our attention - I am not the great "I am" God is the one who deserves to be honoured.

Dear Lord, thank you for our everyday lives. We thank you that you are the God of both the ordinary and the extraordinary. Amen

I HAVE POSTED WATCHMEN ON YOUR WALLS, THEY WILL NEVER BE SILENT DAY OR NIGHT

God speaks every day, he didn't create the world and then go silent. He has continued to communicate with every heartbeat of every living creature since. He speaks his message to us in different ways.

Some of his "speaking" is not a literally audible message. But as the Psalm says "The heavens declare the glory of God; the skies proclaim the work of his hands. Day after day they pour forth speech; night after night they reveal knowledge. They have no speech, they use no words; no sound is heard from them. Yet their voice goes out into all the earth, their words to the ends of the world. "

There is a paradox there. But the point is whether acknowledged or denied God's influence continues. The mystery of our continued life is in his hands.

Sometimes we say, "I don't get God," or "I can't believe in a creator of THIS world." Yet to stand and look at nature's glory is a wonderful thing. To be a parent and hold a newborn baby in your hands is an amazing thing. To know that you have participated in creation is a wonderful thing. Your child has grown cell by cell after it's conception. The miracle of life needs attribution. I attribute it to a loving God.

Even the circulation system for our blood is an amazing thing. Debs and I are big fans of the American TV series "MythBusters" - there was one glorious episode where they were trying to test a movie myth, and Jamie made a circulatory system to go inside a dummy, so they could test how quickly hypothermia comes on. Jamie did a brilliant job with copper tubing and achieved his purpose, but I have to say God's version is a lot neater and lasts a lot longer!

A lot of the reason I write is to try and learn to listen to God and what it is he has to say to me.

For example, I believe that the Bible is God-breathed, inspired with his words for us. So, there are insights to be found in it to guide us. Another way that God influences me is through coincidences with scripture and also the discussion of it with friends and family. Quite often these "coincidences" occur where the same passage comes to my attention in different ways in the same week. It can be that they crop up as much as three or four times. When that happens, I feel that God has a point to emphasise and I need to listen! Like a Watchman in the following passage, it is hard for me to be silent!

> No longer will they call you Deserted, or name your land Desolate. But you will be called Hephzibah, and your land Beulah; for the Lord will take delight in you, and your land will be married. As a young man marries a young woman, so will your Builder marry you; as a bridegroom rejoices over his bride, so will your God rejoice over you. I have posted watchmen on your walls, Jerusalem; they will never be silent day or night. You who call on the Lord , give yourselves no rest... Isaiah 64:8-9 NIV

I find God is not silent. As his creation we need to know he has things to say to us!

> Yet you, Lord , are our Father. We are the clay; you are the potter; we are all the work of your hand. Do not be angry beyond measure, Lord; do not remember our sins forever. Oh, look on us, we pray, for we are all your people.

Both these passages spoke to my heart and reminded me of things that I needed to be aware of and actions I needed to take. Slowly God takes us on a journey.

Watchmen shouldn't be silent by the way! They are to be there on the ramparts watching the winnowing of the Spirit and ready to cry out "Our God saves." We are in a new and different season of the Spirit and if we pay attention to the things of God we should be preparing. I know God has made it clear to me there are some things he expects from me.

This is what he seemed to say to me the other morning; I feel it is for others too. "Extend your boundaries oh faithful ones. Listen to the Lord, ask him to show you who to speak to. Ask him to bless your actions and speak through you in the power of his glorious name. Listen to his voice - let him guide you into the path of righteousness. Let your sins fall behind you as autumn leaves in a fast-flowing stream" Please test my words in your heart.

May Jesus, lead you by the hand to receive healing and wholeness. And May God bless you in the name of the Father, Son, and Holy Spirit. Amen

ARE YOU A GATHERER OR A SCATTERER?

I find I have been doing some thinking recently about the way I live my life. As an unfinished human specimen, I find I still have to be honed! My Debs can confirm that for you if you like!

In particular thinking about something that I stumbled across that Jesus said

> "Anyone who is not for me is really against me; anyone who does not help me gather is really scattering."Matthew 12:30 GNT

Quite a challenging statement that he fired at some Religious nitpickers who had taken issue with him for healing on the Sabbath.

I believe Jesus is talking to people with faith and saying if you are not helping him by gathering people into the "Kingdom of God" you are actually dispersing them.

Jesus came to build the Kingdom of God. This is not a temporal or physical Kingdom. It is a spiritual Kingdom where God reigns in a spirit of loving kindness.

Maybe you don't know that there is such a thing as the Kingdom of God? Let God speak to your heart on this. Love is not a tangible thing. We cannot touch love. Yet it is the most important thing in our life. Pure, true, honest love is what makes us joyful. God is love as it says in the bible. If we found our lives on a foundation of loving actions we become "gatherers" - by our decisions we become builders.

It is better to build. It is better to bless than to curse
Love builds slowly but can be demolished quickly.

Who will rise up for me against the wicked? Who will take a stand for me against evildoers? Psalm 94:16 NIV

"I CALL YOU FRIENDS"

Sometimes Jesus speaks words that cut through our every day, thinking and living. Son of God, Saviour he comes out with words that challenge us. Consider these words from the last supper.

"As the Father has loved me, so have I loved you. Now remain in my love. If you keep my commands, you will remain in my love, just as I have kept my Father's commands and remain in his love. I have told you this so that my joy may be in you and that your joy may be complete. My command is this: Love each other as I have loved you. Greater love has no one than this: to lay down one's life for one's friends. You are my friends if you do what I command. I no longer call you servants, because a servant does not know his master's business. Instead, I have called you friends, for everything that I learned from my Father I have made known to you. You did not choose me, but I chose you and appointed you so that you might go and bear fruit, fruit that will last and so that whatever you ask in my name the Father will give you. This is my command: Love each other."

Those words from Jesus really reach me. They are the extraordinary statement of the new relationship that exists between humankind and God. They are in a way a declaration of love for humankind. After all true friendship is love. There can be a stage in a relationship between two people where it changes and grows, and there is a dawning realisation that it has moved on to a deeper level. Sometimes it is verbalised "we are friends" Similarly this is Jesus speaking out loud, words of friendship" maybe what he and the disciples might have known in their hearts for some time.

"I call you friends" could be thought just a tiny phrase, words to us hidden away in a longer speech that Jesus made at that last meal that he had with his companions before the crucifixion. But I believe that it is very important. The other things that were said at the meal are also important. But they all stem from, or are motivated by, the friendship love expressed. Jesus is the tenderness of God expressed in human form. Jesus fully human yet fully divine is the message of God for all of us. He teaches us that God is not too far away for us to reach. And that His command to love (though difficult) is not impossible. In fact, it is the only thing that can make our lives worthwhile.

Of course, the next thought is how do we respond to the friendship that God is offering us. I was thinking about that and remembered a poem by Kahlil Gibran that I have kept in a little notebook for years.

"and let your best be for your friend.
if he must know the ebb of your tide,
let him know its flood also.
for what is your friend that you should
seek him with hours to kill?
seek him always with hours to live."

That is true friendship - being able to share the good and the bad times. To not shut out a friend is important and a test of friendship. I think if Jesus is a friend I should "seek him always with hours to live" - seek this friend Jesus who has commanded me to love!

Dear Jesus, thank you for your words that challenge us. Help me to respond. We ask your blessing on us in good times and in difficult times. Help us to grow in your love, and rejoice in each other. Amen

DRAW NEAR TO GOD, AND HE WILL DRAW NEAR TO YOU

My thoughts have been elsewhere for a while following a bereavement. But it is time to write again now I think.

The last month has shown me God's capacity to touch our lives even in someone's dying moments. Our God reaches down to touch us when we call to him. He is ever present and ever loving. We make ourselves absent to him sometimes. But that can be mainly through the distraction of everyday life but only very occasionally through deliberate intent.

God is love, and he commands us also to love, to "live a lover's life" in all purity. Sometimes it seems difficult to love. But the commandment is about us changing our way of life to that which makes us more whole.

Love nourishes us in our Spirit.

The commandment to Love is a command to live out love in our lives. To love God, to love our neighbour, to love ourselves. Although it is a commandment, it is actually "best policy" advice from our creator about how to have a full and happy life. Choose love, and you will find joy and peace. Choose to hate, and you will feel forever jagged. It is a daily choice.

Think about Ecclesiasticus (Sirach) words: "If you wish, you can keep the commandments, to behave faithfully is within your power. He has set fire and water before you; put out your hand to whichever you prefer. Man has life and death before him; whichever a man likes better will be given him. For vast is the wisdom of the Lord; he is almighty and all-seeing. His eyes are on those that fear him. He notes every action of man. He never commanded anyone to be Godless he has given no one permission to sin."

Peace to your hearts this day! My prayer is that you may be blessed this day to the core of your being. That God will be evident to you. May you come to know peace. Amen

FOLLOW JESUS

I have been thinking of how Jesus called Matthew out of his tax booth. See Matthew 9: 9-13.

Matthew left his job to follow Jesus. He didn't work out a period of notice. His encounter with Jesus was enough to knock him off the normal course of his life. Bless him, he was a tax collector, in those days fairly despised individuals known for their corruption and for taking an extra cut from those that they were collecting from. It says in the JB translation that he was by the 'Customs House'. This is a mistranslation. He was by his tax collector's booth! This was a portable construction that was set up where he was collecting his tax. All a bit more vulnerable than we at first think. He must have been challenged by Jesus to leave this and also torn. Do I hang on to the money or follow the Holy Man? Well, he became one of the twelve - so he must have opted for the life-changing option to follow Jesus. What would we do I wonder? What would I do - if the Messiah came walking by?

To encounter Jesus at that time was something that knocked people off the normal course of their lives. I believe this was because Jesus personality was so arresting that you had to stop in your tracks and say to yourself. Who is he? Is he for real? What is he offering?

Well, what Jesus offers is something that is contrary to the material world's values. The Good News is something for our spirit, something for the inner man or woman. That lifts us up and alters our lives and changes them for the better. To live outside Christianity is to live a life without hope. To live as a Christian implies a commitment to change.

Yes, Jesus comes to sinners, tax collectors and prostitutes to the shock and dismay of the Pharisees, but it is so that he can bring the healing power of God's love. As he says, he comes as a doctor into their lives. He doesn't feast with the Matthews of this world to pick up tax collecting hints. He doesn't feast with prostitutes in order to pimp. He is at the feast because he has something of real value to give he is offering rescue. REAL RESCUE.

To the Pharisees, he says 'Go and learn the meaning of the words what I want is mercy, not sacrifice.'

The irony is that the Pharisees were sinners too. The difference between them and the others was that they didn't know it. They were too busy looking at other people's lives to assess their own.

If you look at the passage again, you will see that Jesus is ministering to everyone including the Pharisees.

This is why his ministry is so affecting. It speaks to everyone and to us - even now across time. The quote he offers the Pharisees is from the Bible. From the book of Hosea. Which says, 'What I want is love, not sacrifice; knowledge of God, not holocausts.'

That is interesting, isn't it? In the time before Jesus, they used to try and appease God by killing and burning animals as a sin offering in the hope that this would put them right with God. Hosea says that God doesn't want this kind of material response. He wants us to change so that we love more. This requires a change of heart - are we ready?

I have come to realise my life is empty without love."

Dear Lord, help me to leave the things I do that are the old way of living. Allow me to follow you. Please give me the spiritual strength to do so.

Amen

LEAD A LOVER'S LIFE

I had the privilege yesterday of being on the door at church while two baptisms were going on. These were two adults who have chosen life in Christ.

It seemed that everyone at church yesterday was moved by the "testimony" or life story that was shared by Gavin and Shirley.

There is something that brings people to that kind of decision point.

For some people, it is the discovery that there is a spiritual side to life. That we are body, soul and spirit. That our hearts are hungry. Thirsting for the things of God.

We have a free will of course. But God through his son Jesus and through the prophets has invited us to "choose life" instead of "choosing death" - this is about choosing life in the Holy Spirit. Instead of choosing things that kill our spirit.

Some of our Feet for the Street visitors went through the glass door, so they could see and hear things better. My side of the door was a bit muffled. So I missed some of what was said.

I found myself remembering an email sent to me by a friend. He sent me the following verses and said that he had felt prompted by God to do so.

> So this is my prayer: that your love will flourish and that you will not only love much but well. Learn to love appropriately. You need to use your head and test your feelings so that your love is sincere and intelligent, not sentimental gush. Live a lover's life, circumspect and exemplary, a life Jesus will be proud of: bountiful in fruits from the soul, making Jesus Christ attractive to all, getting everyone involved in the glory and praise of God. Philippians 1:9-11

As we go through life different phrases, get added to the interior soundtrack of our lives. Some are the trigger for jokes we have with the family or friends. Silly little phrases that still make us crease up, and we have half-forgotten when they were first used and why.

Some have a more useful role as almost "self-talk" little reminders and way markers that are good for us.

For me, the phrase "Live a Lover's Life" has become a way marker. A signpost for my life. Reminding me to keep on track. To always choose life, to choose life. To put to death the way of hate.

The above passage is very important to me it is a 'way marker' for me telling me 'go this way follow the way of wisdom!' I go back to it quite regularly and read it and ask myself "am I doing that?" Of course, I wouldn't say I ever succeed in loving like that, but it gives me inspiration and a point to aim at.

Dear God, help me to recognise the things that are good for me. Help me to find the things and people who can help me. Send your Spirit to teach me, love. May I be tender-hearted towards other people. Amen

ON LOVE!

Valentine's Day is a day for celebrating love. Artificially selected by the makers of greetings cards it strikes terror in the heart of those dying to express love for someone. I well remember as a young lad the angst of buying and sending my first valentine card anonymously and then being surprised at not getting a response. Doh! I was so diffident then that she probably didn't even know I existed.

But let's think about love today. I can't help smiling to myself having written that. The definition of love itself is nigh impossible, but we know it when we see it. One saint put it "to love is to will the good of another", and that is my preferred working definition. C S Lewis adds to that by pointing out that there are four types of love in his book The Four Loves.

Eros
Philia
Agape
Storge

Today's love celebration is all about eros love. Passionate love declared! Passionate love acted upon! Passionate love felt!

It's interesting that the Bible describes God's love vividly in all four ways. It's like God wants us to fully comprehend that he loves in stereo using four speakers instead of dreary old mono.

They say that when the Holy Spirit comes into our life, he makes our hearts more tender for one another. We start to, more frequently, desire good for other people.

On the way to the station this morning I remembered that God is described sometimes as a jealous lover. He wants us to love him wholeheartedly in the school of love. We can then express our love more perfectly with others. He doesn't want us to love, or make, other Gods. He is jealous in that sense. He is jealously angry when we seek the face of another God.

He wants us to be bold and courageous in all our loving. He doesn't want us to be watered down and insipid. Or for us to dilute our love with lust. He wants us to be completely sincere too and not lead people on if we can't return their love.

Think about this

> Let love and faithfulness never leave you; bind them around your neck, write them on the tablet of your heart. Proverbs 3:3 NIV

Dear Lord, I pray a blessing on this day. So that whether single or in a relationship, our love is blessed. Amen

BIDDEN OR UNBIDDEN GOD IS PRESENT

I have been thinking a lot recently about the nature of God. I think he is far less harsh than people give him credit for. And far more creative. And far more elusive. I will try not to machine gun you with quotes, but I want to explain that I have some basis for making these statements.

The bible is a kind of love story collection of writings about God. It ranges from stories about God in a huff, and believe me lovers do get in a huff sometimes, to accounts of God the tender-hearted loving creator of each one of us, with all sorts of tones in between. It's easy to get hung up on one aspect. But to see God properly needs an understanding that he or she is very elusive. "We can't put God in a box" as the saying goes.

God is just there! Existing! Regardless of any action, we might take, but at the same time, he wants to call us into a love relationship.

Some Australian friends used to have a bronze plaque in their Hall. It fascinated me, and it had the words on it "Bidden or unbidden, God is present" which apparently is a translation of a Latin saying. It is a beautiful reminder that God is like a very persistent lover, who persists in making overtures to the beloved regardless of how they are received. Persistent, foolish perhaps if we turn our backs on him. But God is so caring for us that he continues long after a human lover would have given up. He provides our earthly life. Oh, that we could but realise. "in him we live and move and have our being" as the apostle Paul puts it.

Have a pause and a think over the words in this passage for example:

> Dear friends, let us love one another, for love comes from God. Everyone who loves has been born of God and knows God. Whoever does not love does not know God, because God is love.
> 1 John 4:7-8 NIV

That was written by John, one of Jesus closest companions.

I got in a taxi the other day and got into conversation quite easily with the driver. We ended up discussing that very passage. I asked the driver to imagine how he felt on seeing his own children when they were born. God's delight in us, his children, is greater and more continuing.

Today I invite you to remember God your creator. Let him speak gently into your life. Ask him to bless you and change your heart.

> *And they were calling to one another: "Holy, holy, holy is the Lord Almighty; the whole earth is full of his glory." Isaiah 6:3 NIV*

DEPART IN SILENCE!

Let's start with an unapologetic trip down memory lane.

I have been thinking recently about the use of and meaning of silence in church and prayer groups. At men's prayer group we have been experimenting with silence in a group setting.

Depart in silence! That's what the instructions say for the Catholic liturgy on Maundy Thursday. At St Gertie's, in the 1990s we had a bit of a campaign to try and make that happen. It's not because we were trying to "harsh anyone's buzz", but it's just extremely fitting to have a reverent or even stunned silence after you have determinedly remembered and tried to make yourself present at the last meal Jesus had before his death. When you consider the enormity of the situation for the disciples. The mixture of the Thanksgiving meal, Jesus talking like he was going to die and Judas betrayal. The instruction should say "depart in stunned silence." But I forget the number of times we explained to people if you are being true to the events you don't have a hymn at this point. You should leave the church in total silence or stay praying until midnight. It's one of the times where there should be a sense of grief almost in a church setting. A time where there should be no chitter-chatter in the church afterwards. Reverent silence. But does modern man or woman do reverence? Of course, some do!

Silence can be surprisingly instructive if we can dare to expose ourselves to it. But watch out! God can speak in the silence, so if you weren't planning for that to happen, it could be disconcerting. I have experimented with silence in my prayer times and found that sometimes it can be energising or even powerful. There are different kinds of silence. For me, silent prayer usually comes after I have said some psalms and I have set my heart to listen to God. There then follows minutes of what I think of as 'struggling silence.' It is the struggle not to stop and think about something else like the shopping or the dripping tap. Or the cat. If I can get beyond the struggle, I can reach a stage of contented silence. Where "God looks at me, and I look at him" - as friends, we don't always need to talk to each other. This is content silence. If you are really fortunate you can then go beyond this and God will speak. Not audibly of course. The God speaking silences are more frequent once you make yourself available. Today in the silence God asked one question "did you refuse to prophesy in my name?" His questions can be disturbing. Sometimes he can tell you that he loves you. It's not all challenge. He is, after all, a tender-hearted God.

Sometimes I pray in tongues in the prayer time. This can help. It can lead to one of those loaded silences where God is present in all of his glory.

I don't normally talk about this stuff. But I think sometimes there is a time to share what's going through your head. Prayer is like an acorn. Hard to tap into. But once the right conditions are reached. Growth happens. The picture is of an acorn we found in the back garden. Your prayer life can lead to growth like this!

> James 1:21-25 NIV Humbly accept the word planted in you, which can save you. Do not merely listen to the word, and so deceive yourselves. Do what it says. Anyone who listens to the word but does not do what it says is like someone who looks at his face in a mirror and, after looking at himself, goes away and immediately forgets what he looks like. But whoever looks intently into the perfect law that gives freedom, and continues in it-not forgetting what they have heard, but doing it-they will be blessed in what they do.

*Dear God, let me go deeper into your heart. Help me to hunger for the peace of Christ. Send your Holy Spirit to renew my life. Let me welcome you!
Amen*

THE GIFT OF FAITH

Lately, I have found myself involved in a few conversations where I have been prompted to remember how I came to believe in God.

I "caught" God as a young man. Not caught like you catch a virus. But God found me, and I started to understand why he was searching for me and wanted me to know about him. I could have denied his presence. I could have pushed him away, but I didn't. I am so glad because when I found him, and he found me, he changed my life. I know that he meets the darkness in me with his light. He moves me to love, whereas the things of this world can easily move me to hate. God the ever living, ever loving creator of the world, wants to be in a relationship with me and also seeks you just as avidly.

I am praying this morning, as you read this for the gift of faith for you. Just as God hovered over the waters, breathing life, I ask him to breathe faith into your being.

Looking back on my life I can see that certain people did this for me. I know my mother, for example, had carried on praying for me after I had opted out of going to church with her. In my agnostic phase, she never gave up praying for me. And then there were certain chance meetings that I had with people that led to decision points. Yes, there were more than one! Certain people were sent to stand in the gap between God and me. To help me get my head around what was going on.

Our life isn't just about our flesh and blood and our human desires. There is a Spiritual side to life that we sometimes ignore or push below the surface although we can readily believe in spiritual evil we are less ready to believe in good.

One of the very first people to have an encounter was a shepherd called Moses. He had a very clear encounter with God. Not many of us will have experiences like that. But we can have our own small encounters with God which can be just as convincing. Times when we feel the presence of God.

Moses is a biblical hero, but he didn't start out that way. In fact, if you read his life story, you discover he was a murderer. Someone who did something very wrong before he encountered God and managed to get his life back.

When Moses meets God, it is one of the first occasions that we know of where God speaks directly to a man. As I said Moses at the time is living as a Shepherd. A shepherd's life is very solitary, and a lot of time is spent watching the sheep, and the weather, and the countryside, a life full of contemplation.

One day Moses sees a burning bush. It's a strange fire because it is not consuming the bush.

He hears God calling to him from within the bush, saying "Moses! Moses! "So Moses thought, "I will go over and see this strange sight--why the bush does not burn up."

When the Lord saw that he had gone over to look, God called to him from within the bush, "Moses! Moses!"

And Moses said, "Here I am."

"Do not come any closer," God said. "Take off your sandals, for the place where you are standing is holy ground."

Then he said, "I am the God of your father, the God of Abraham, the God of Isaac and the God of Jacob."

At this, Moses hid his face, because he was afraid to look at God. The Lord said, "I have indeed seen the misery of my people in Egypt. I have heard them crying out because of their slave drivers, and I am concerned about their suffering. So I have come down to rescue them from the hand of the Egyptians and to bring them up out of that land into a good and spacious land, a land flowing with milk and honey--the home of the Canaanites, Hittites, Amorites, Perizzites, Hivites and Jebusites. And now the cry of the Israelites has reached me, and I have seen the way the Egyptians are oppressing them. So now, go. I am sending you to Pharaoh to bring my people the Israelites out of Egypt."

But Moses said to God, "Who am I that I should go to Pharaoh and bring the Israelites out of Egypt?" And God said, "I will be with you. And this will be the sign to you that it is I who have sent you: When you have brought the people out of Egypt, you will worship God on this mountain."

Moses said to God, "Suppose I go to the Israelites and say to them, 'The God of your fathers has sent me to you,' and they ask me, 'What is his name?' Then what shall I tell them?"

God said to Moses, " I am who I am. This is what you are to say to the Israelites: ' I am has sent me to you.' " God also said to Moses, "Say to the Israelites, 'The Lord , the God of your fathers--the God of Abraham, the God of Isaac and the God of Jacob--has sent me to you.' "This is my name forever, the name you shall call me from generation to generation.

Dear God, increase the gift of faith within me. I pray that in your own way you may be present in my life to bless me and also my family. Amen

"ALLOW GOD TO HOLD YOU TIGHT "

Once in the big silence at Men's Prayer Group when we turned our mind to God.

I got this image of a drill. A workman was holding a drill and drilling into the wall. The drill bit was wobbling all over the place because the chuck hadn't been tightened properly. I got a sense that things had been very shaky with me that week because I hadn't been held tight. I thought I am like that drill bit. The words "allow God to hold you tight" came to me and I felt certain it was him reminding me to allow him to tighten the chuck on my life. To let him drill using me! Scary and it means going deeper into prayer. Deeper into discovering what God wants. I must. I must "allow God to hold me tight" - it's about surrender. Do I dare?

"If you judge people you have no time to love them" Mother Teresa

◆ ◆ ◆

Let us shout aloud to the Rock of our salvation!
(Psalm 95:1)

ON PILGRIMAGE

> Psalm 84:5 says "Blessed are those whose strength is in you, whose hearts are set on pilgrimage."

I hope that this book has encouraged you in your faith and that you will be strong and happy in your life, that you will be blessed.

In a way, people of faith are constantly on pilgrimage. St Paul in his letter to the Hebrews speaks among others of Abel, Enoch, Noah, Abraham, Isaac and Jacob, who are described as 'strangers and pilgrims on the earth'.

'Strangers' literally means foreigners, people of a different culture and language. 'Pilgrims' are those who live in a foreign land, away from their own people.

In the Bible, the pilgrim word implies a journey – or even travelling home. Biblical pilgrims live in another country alongside the resident community, but they do not fully integrate. They are 'alongsiders', soon to go home. They may accomplish great things for the benefit of the country in which they live (as Joseph did), but they never cease to be pilgrims.

I invite you to set your heart on a pilgrimage today! We should travel light. Shedding our emotional baggage through healing and jettisoning our cumbersome physical luggage. The courageous ones do "take nothing for the journey" for indeed our true wealth is in our faith. But whatever our circumstances God will hear our cry to him and answer it.

IF YOU LIKED THIS BOOK

- If you were given it please consider reviewing it on www.amazon.co.uk or on your country's Amazon site, or alternatively on www.goodreads.com
- Please also consider gifting the Amazon Kindle version to a friend. This can be done for the price equivalent of a cup of coffee.
- Any reviews you leave encourage other readers when making their book choices.

1

Printed in Great Britain
by Amazon